The Freshwater Angler

FLY FISHING
Strategies & Tactics

● ● ● ● ● ● ● ● ● ● ● ● ● ● ● ● ● ●

How to Hook and Land More Trout

Creative Publishing
international

Chanhassen, Minnesota

**Creative Publishing
international**

Copyright © 2006 by Creative Publishing international, Inc.
18705 Lake Drive East
Chanhassen, MN 55317
1-800-328-3895
www.creativepub.com

President/CEO: Ken Fund
Vice President/Publisher: Linda Ball
Vice President/Retail Sales & Marketing: Kevin Haas

FLY FISHING STRATEGIES & TACTICS

Executive Editor, Outdoor Group: Barbara Harold
Creative Director: Brad Springer
Page Layout: Pamela Griffith
Production Manager: Laura Hokkanen

Contributing Photographer:
Bill Lindner Photography; www.blpstudio.com
  ©Bill Lindner Photography: pp. 151, 154-155

Contributing Illustrator:
Joseph R. Tomelleri; www.americanfishes.com
  ©Joseph R. Tomelleri: pp. 28-29, 30-31

Printing: R. R. Donnelley
10   9   8   7   6   5   4   3   2   1

Library of Congress Cataloging-in-Publication Data

Fly fishing strategies & tactics : how to hook and land more trout / by
the editors of Creative Publishing International.
    p. cm.
  Includes index.
  ISBN 1-58923-219-4 (soft cover)
  1. Trout fishing.   2. Fly fishing.   I. Title: Fly fishing strategies and tactics.
  II. Creative Publishing International.
  SH687.F582 2005
  799.17'57—dc22   2005002748

CONTENTS

INTRODUCTION

AMONG PEOPLE WHO FISH WITH FLY RODS, TROUT ARE MORE POPULAR THAN ANY OTHER SPECIES. In streams located across the United States and throughout the world, interest in fly fishing for trout is at an all-time high, and the need for clear, concise information has increased proportionally. This book, *Fly Fishing Strategies and Tactics*, focuses on the

most reliable, time-tested information a fly angler will need when wading the trout streams of the world.

The first section will help you select and understand the gear you will need when fishing for trout in streams.

In the second section, we will teach you the basic knots for making leaders, connecting them to the fly line and tying on flies. Knot tying is a skill that must be learned by a fly angler.

Then, you'll learn one of the most important skills in fly fishing: casting. In this section, we'll explain the function of each important basic cast and, using step-by-step photography, show you exactly how to make it. In following chapters, we will show you more-specialized casts that can be used when fishing in a variety of different situations.

Before you can use any technique effectively, it is important that you understand the trout, the fish's natural surroundings and the foods that it eats. The third chapter begins with

4

an explanation of the trout's senses, helping you to understand why trout react to circumstances in the way they do. This chapter also will help you assess a stream's fishing potential by explaining how environmental factors – such as water fertility, water temperature and current speed – affect the number and size of trout a stream can produce. We also show you how to recognize the basic riffle-run-pool configuration of a trout stream and how to identify the different types of trout lies. With this understanding you'll spend your time fishing where the fish are located, not in empty water. And we explain what foods trout eat and how they feed, so you'll know what type of fly to use. At the end of this section is information on different ways to check for the types of foods that trout are feeding on in a stream.

The subsurface techniques section details the most effective methods for fishing trout along the bottom of a stream or in the mid-depths. You'll learn which techniques work best in what water types and how to select the right equipment for each method. Finally, using detailed step-by-step photos and diagrams, we'll show you how to perfectly execute each technique, including any special-purpose casts.

The following section on surface techniques begins with short sections on equipment, seeing the fly and the general techniques used for fishing flies on the surface. This information will provide you with the background information needed before you learn the techniques for upstream, cross-stream and downstream presentations. In each of these presentations, we will show you the casts and line-handling techniques used when approaching a fish. And we will show you how to fish surface flies blind – when there is no visible or rising fish.

This book will help you learn or improve your fly-fishing skills and presentations. It tells you the important information needed to select equipment, tie knots, cast, analyze a trout stream, present a fly to a trout and successfully catch it. Studying this book and tailoring your techniques to suit the water and the fish's behavior is the first step to becoming a complete fly fisherman.

1

FLY-FISHING
EQUIPMENT

Fly Rods

The fly rod is the single most important tool in fly fishing. It is used to cast the fly line, which, in turn, delivers the leader and the fly. The rod is also important in controlling the line on or in the water, and in playing a fish once it is hooked.

Fly rods come in a wide range of styles and prices, depending on the type of fishing you plan to do and on your budget. When choosing a fly rod, consider material, action, length and weight designation.

MATERIAL. What a rod is made of determines its weight, cost and how it performs on the water.

The earliest fly rods were made from woods such as ash, hickory, willow and greenheart, a South American hardwood. These long, heavy rods were used to place, rather than cast, a fly.

By the 1850s, a number of American rodbuilders were experimenting with slender strips of split bamboo glued together to form a single blank. Bamboo, or split-cane, rods were remarkably strong, yet flexible. Consequently, they could be made lighter for their length than earlier wood rods.

But bamboo rods were expensive and required regular maintenance, such as revarnishing, and careful storage to prevent warping. To solve these problems, a number of rodbuilders began to impregnate the bamboo with synthetic resins.

GRAPHITE rods are made from sheets of carbon-fiber material wrapped around a tapered steel form, called a mandrel.

Fiberglass rods were introduced in the late 1940s and quickly eclipsed bamboo in popularity. They were cheaper and more durable, and could be mass produced. These early fiberglass rods were made from solid blanks, so they lacked rigidity, resulting in unpredictable casting dynamics. By the early 1950s, however, rodbuilders were wrapping fiberglass cloth around a tapered steel form, or mandrel, to produce a hollow blank. This method greatly increased rigidity while reducing the overall weight of the finished fly rod.

In the 1960s, aerospace engineers developed graphite, a carbon-fiber material which, like fiberglass, was available as a cloth. But graphite is much stronger for its weight than fiberglass, giving it a higher stiffness-to-weight ratio, or modulus. As a result, graphite rods are lighter and thinner than bamboo or glass and produce higher line speeds for greater casting distance.

Graphite eventually replaced glass, and by the early 1980s, few fiberglass rods were being produced. Today, over 95 percent of all fly rods are graphite. But some manufacturers still add fiberglass to their graphite rods for durability, and a handful continue to build high-quality, all-glass rods. Bamboo rods are still made in limited numbers and remain the finest examples of the rodmaker's craft.

ACTION. There is no common definition of fly-rod action, and most manufacturers do not even designate the action of their rods. But action is important and is determined by two different characteristics. The first is how and where the rod bends under a load (right), as it does when casting a line. The second is how quickly it recovers from a bend, or dampens. Both of these characteristics are determined by what the rod is made of, its modulus and its taper, or the way in which the rod narrows from butt to tip.

A rod with a fast recovery rate is almost always preferable to one that recovers slowly. But recovery rates vary among individual rods and rods from different manufacturers, and there is no standard method of measurement.

LENGTH. Most fly rods fall into the 7 1/2 - to 9-foot range. Rods shorter than 7 1/2 feet are popular with light-line or small-creek enthusiasts, while rods over 9 feet are used in large-river situations.

WEIGHT. Not to be confused with how much a rod weighs, the weight designation of a fly rod describes the size fly line the rod is designed to cast most effectively. In other words, a 4-weight rod is designed to cast a 4-weight line. Fly rods range in weight from 1 to 15, but the majority of stream trout rods fall in the 3- to 8-weight range.

PARTS OF A FLY ROD

Butt
Reel seat
Grip
Hookkeeper
Ferrule (female)

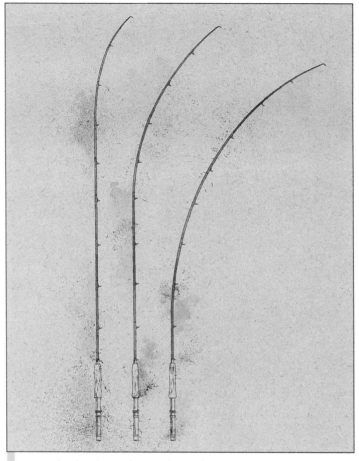

A ROD that bends mainly near the tip during a cast is described as fast action (left); one that bends into the midsection, medium action (middle); and one that bends into the butt section, slow action (right). Fast-dampening rods also have a fast action; slow-dampening, slow action.

Stripping guide

Ferrule (male)

Snake guides

Tip-top

Popular Grip Styles & Reel Seats

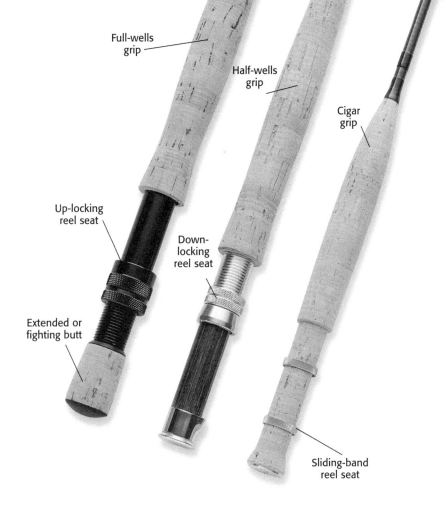

Full-wells grip

Half-wells grip

Cigar grip

Up-locking reel seat

Down-locking reel seat

Extended or fighting butt

Sliding-band reel seat

GRIP STYLE. How a rod feels in your hand depends in part on the design of the grip. One that is too fat or too thin can make the whole rod feel awkward. There are as many grip styles as there are rodmakers; however, a few styles have become standard and are offered on most production rods. The most popular styles are the cigar, half-wells and full-wells (p. 12).

The cigar grip is often used on lighter rods, for a more delicate feel; heavier rods generally have a full-wells grip, which is flared at both ends. The half-wells is flared at only one end and used on intermediate-weight rods. A front flare provides extra leverage for your thumb; a rear flare allows room for the reel foot on up-locking reel seats (p. 12). Select a grip that fits your hand and feels comfortable when casting.

REEL SEAT. Some light rods have sliding-band reel seats, with lightweight rings or bands to hold the foot of the reel. Medium and heavy rods usually have up-locking seats, which are more secure but require a thicker grip, because one foot of the reel slides under the grip. Down-locking seats are losing popularity, mainly because the reel is at the very end of the rod, making it difficult to place the butt against your body for extra fighting leverage.

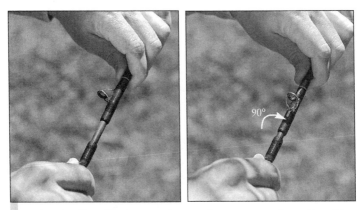

ASSEMBLE fly rod by inserting butt section into top section with guides 90° out of alignment (left). Twist sections gently, while aligning guides, until tight (right). If you push the sections together straight, it will wear a groove that can cause the rod sections to accidentally come apart. To take rod apart, simply twist sections 90° while pulling.

Reels

Some experts will tell you that a reel is simply a place to store line; but that's a little like saying a car's brake pedal is just a place to rest your foot. Today's reels perform a variety of functions and are far more sophisticated than they appear. Here are some considerations in fly-reel selection:

DRAG. A good, adjustable drag slows a running trout and prevents spool overrun. The larger the fish, the more important the drag becomes.

The most simple and common type of drag is the ratchet-and-pawl. An adjustable spring keeps the pawl pressed against the ratchet, making an audible click.

Disc-style drags perform like the disc brakes on a car, using the smooth friction of one large surface against another.

Many reels have an exposed spool rim, which allows you to apply additional drag tension by pressing your open hand against the rim, a technique called palming.

MATERIAL. Fly reels are made from a variety of materials, including aluminum and graphite. Aluminum reels are the most common and come in all price ranges. Reels machined from a single block of aluminum alloy, called bar stock, can cost up to ten times as much as those stamped from sheet alloy. Some aluminum reels are anodized for additional corrosion resistance.

Graphite reels are lightweight and offer a low-cost alternative to metal, but they are not as durable and their parts do not fit as precisely.

ACTION. A reel's action describes the rate at which it retrieves line. On a single-action reel, the most common type, the spool turns once for each turn of the handle, for a 1:1 retrieve ratio. Single-actions are light, durable and have few moving parts to fail. A multiplying reel has additional gearing that causes the spool to turn more than once for each turn of the handle, usually from 1.5 to 3 times, for a retrieve ratio of 1.5:1 to 3:1. Multiplying reels are frequently used in situations where you need to take up line in a hurry.

DRIVE. Most reels are direct-drive, meaning that the handle rotates with the spool in either direction. But if a fish makes a fast run, the spinning handle can take the skin off your knuckles. Anti-reverse reels employ a clutch mechanism, which keeps the handle from spinning backward when a fish takes out line.

SIZE AND CAPACITY. The reel you choose should be designed to hold the size fly line you've selected with ample capacity for backing material (p. 22). The larger the fish you're after, the greater the capacity you'll need.

REEL-CARE TIPS

LUBRICATE reel periodically to keep it operating smoothly. Choose a lubricant designed for reels.

WASH a used reel with fresh water and soap to prevent corrosion. Dry reel thoroughly before storing.

PARTS OF A REEL

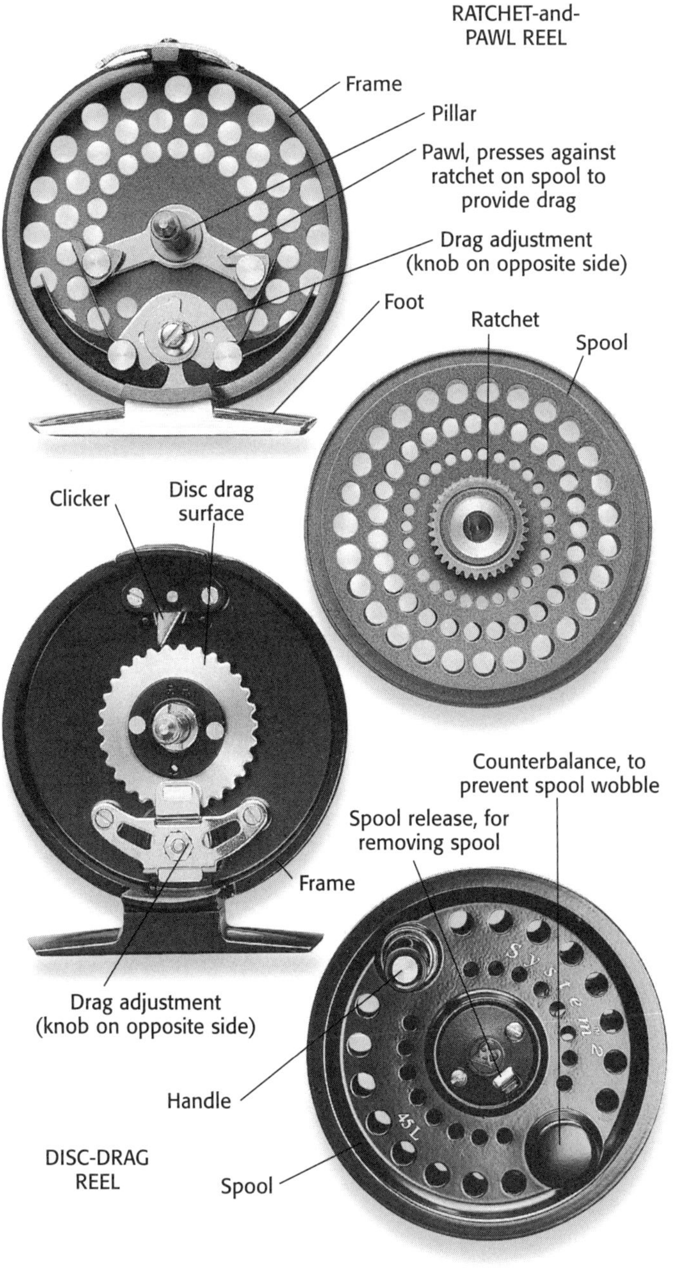

RATCHET-and-
PAWL REEL

Frame

Pillar

Pawl, presses against
ratchet on spool to
provide drag

Drag adjustment
(knob on opposite side)

Foot

Ratchet

Spool

Clicker

Disc drag
surface

Counterbalance, to
prevent spool wobble

Spool release, for
removing spool

Frame

Drag adjustment
(knob on opposite side)

Handle

DISC-DRAG
REEL

Spool

Fly Lines

The fly line distinguishes fly fishing from all other forms of fishing and makes it possible to cast an essentially weightless fly. The weight of the line bends, or loads, the rod, propelling the line, leader and fly.

Fly lines, which are typically 80 to 105 feet long, come in many weights, tapers and colors. Some are designed to float; others to sink at varying rates and to different depths. Still others are a combination of floating and sinking line segments. Your choice of line depends primarily on the size of your fly, the distance you want to cast it and the depth at which you want to present it. When choosing a fly line, consider:

WEIGHT. Besides determining what size fly you can cast, line weight also affects the distance of your cast and the delicacy of your presentation. For best casting performance, be sure your line is matched to your rod.

Lines range in weight from size 1 (the lightest) to size 12. You can buy special-purpose lines as heavy as size 15. The majority of lines used for fishing trout in streams fall between size 3 and size 8. Line-weight designation is based on the weight (measured in grains) of the first 30 feet of the fly line.

Lightweight lines (sizes 1 to 4) are best for delicate presentations of tiny flies at short distances.

Mediumweight lines (sizes 5 to 7) cast well in most fishing situations and will handle a wide range of fly sizes.

Heavyweight lines (sizes 8 and above) are suited for casting large flies to big fish. They are recommended for long-distance casting or punching a fly into the wind.

TAPER. Variation in thickness of the line's coating along its length determines its taper, which dictates how it performs in the air and on the water. Following are the most common tapers:

Double-taper (DT) lines have a long belly section tapering to identical front and rear sections. Double-tapers are popular for light-line trout fishing where a delicate presentation is required. They cast well at short to medium distances and are ideal for roll casting (p. 58). Because both ends are identical, double-taper lines can be reversed when one end wears out, extending line life.

Weight-forward (WF) lines are designed with most of the weight in the first 30 feet, tapering quickly to a long, thin section called running line. Weight-forwards cast farther than double-tapers, are better for casting in the wind and are a good choice for beginners. But they do not roll-cast as well as double-tapers.

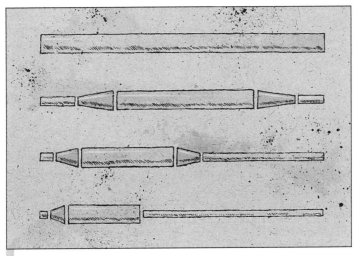

LINE TAPERS include: (top) level line, (upper middle) double-taper line, (lower middle) weight-forward line and (bottom) shooting taper, or shooting head, with separate running line.

Shooting tapers (ST) have a short, compact head that is attached to a separate monofilament or coated-Dacron running line. The head easily pulls the thin running line through the guides, enabling you to cast very long distances – over 100 feet. But the head lacks delicacy and accuracy, and the running line tends to tangle easily. In stream trout fishing a shooting taper is not used or needed in most of the situations encountered. It is utilized only in very specialized presentation techniques such as the deep streamer swing (p. 150).

Level lines (L) have a consistent diameter along their entire length. Although inexpensive, they are difficult to cast and rarely used.

BUOYANCY. Modern fly lines are carefully designed to float high or sink at a predictable rate. The right buoyancy depends on the type of fly you are using and how deep the fish are feeding.

Floating lines (F), the most popular type, have a coating impregnated with tiny air bubbles. Ideal for presenting dry flies, they are easy to cast and mend (p. 60), and won't pull the fly below the surface. They allow you to pick up and recast a fly quickly and easily.

Floating lines can be used for fishing subsurface flies by adding weight to the leader or fly, but in situations where the line prevents your fly from getting deep enough, a sinking line may be a better choice.

Sinking lines (S) vary in density, depending on the amount of lead or tungsten particles in the coating. Some lines are only a little denser than water, causing them to sink slowly. Others are denser and sink quickly, allowing you to fish at depths of 25 feet or more. With a sinking line, the entire length sinks, so the line can be difficult to control in the air and in the water, and you must retrieve most of the line before you can cast again.

Sink-tip, or floating/sinking lines (F/S), combine a long floating belly with a 5- to 25-foot sinking tip. The floating portion lets you control the line on the surface, while the sinking tip gets your fly down at varying rates, depending on line density. Sink-tip lines are easier to cast than full-sinking lines, but won't get as deep.

COLOR. Fly-line color is a matter of personal preference. Light-colored or fluorescent lines are a good choice for beginners, because they're easy to see on the water and in the air. Some anglers believe these colors spook the fish, but, in most cases, fish do not see the line because of the leader. Sinking lines come in darker browns and greens, making them less visible under water. The sinking portion of a sink-tip line is also dark, but the floating part is light-colored, to help you detect strikes.

BACKING

Without backing, a big trout could easily run out your entire fly line. Backing gives you the extra line you need to control the fish and connects your fly line to your reel. It also fills up the spool so you can reel in line more quickly.

The most common backing material is braided Dacron in 20- to 30-pound test. The average reel holds up to 150 yards of backing.

HOW TO ADD BACKING

SECURE backing to reel with an arbor knot (p. 41), then wind on desired amount of backing directly from the spool, keeping tension on the backing so it winds on tightly. The amount of backing needed depends on its diameter, the size of the reel and the weight and type of fly line. Check the instructions that come with your reel for specific backing recommendations.

LINE-CARE TIPS

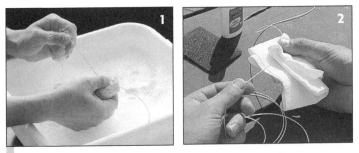

(1)CLEAN fly line with mild soap and water to remove dirt. Do not use abrasives, which can damage line coating. (2)TREAT cleaned line with a protectant to maintain plastic coating and help line shoot smoothly through guides.

Fly Leaders & Tippets

The leader creates a nearly invisible connection between the heavy fly line and the fly. It also transfers the energy of the cast smoothly and efficiently, and helps give the fly a lifelike action on or in the water. These issues are important in leader selection:

MATERIAL. Until the 1950s, fly leaders were made from silkworm gut, which was strong and had low visibility, but became stiff and brittle when dry. Gut leaders required overnight soaking to make them supple enough for fishing.

Modern leaders come in a variety of man-made materials, which require far less care. They are available in a wide range of diameters, strengths, colors and hardnesses.

Nylon monofilament, by far the most popular leader material, is inexpensive, durable and nearly invisible, with excellent knot strength. But monofilament breaks down quickly in sunlight and will absorb water, causing it to weaken.

Braided nylon, though not as popular as it once was, cushions the shock of a hook set and turns over smoothly. But braided nylon is more visible than mono and, like mono, it absorbs water.

Polyvinylidene fluoride (PVDF) leader material, commonly called "fluorocarbon," is even less visible in water than nylon, because its refractive properties, or the way it bends light rays, more closely match the properties of water. It has 50 percent more abrasion resistance than nylon, but

PARTS OF A LEADER

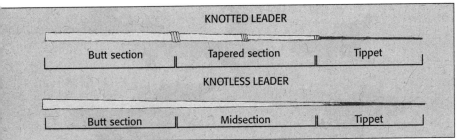

LEADERS can be divided into three sections. The butt section makes up about 35 to 45 percent of the length; the midsection (tapered section in knotted leader), 40 to 55 percent; and the tippet section, 10 to 25 percent.

50 percent less stretch, requiring a more gentle hook set to prevent break-offs with light tippets. PVDF is not affected by sunlight and will not absorb water. However, it costs more and has poorer knot strength than mono.

TAPER. Most leaders taper from a relatively thick butt section to a fine tippet. As a result, the leader turns over easily and presents only the narrow-diameter tippet to the trout.

There are two types of tapered leaders: knotted and knotless. A knotted, or compound, leader is made up of several sections of different-diameter line, tied end to end. You can buy knotted leaders pretied, or tie your own to suit your type of fishing.

Knotless leaders taper gradually and may be a better choice for beginners or those unsure of their knots. They work well for fishing around vegetation, because there are no knots to catch weeds. They turn over well and are simple to use, but you may need to add tippet material when numerous fly changes shorten your leader.

LENGTH. The length of your leader depends on the type of fly and line you are using. When fishing dry flies, always use the longest leader you can comfortably cast, usually 7½ to 12 feet. For subsurface flies and sinking lines, use leaders shorter than 9 feet.

TIPPET DIAMETER. A tippet's diameter is measured using a system developed in the days of silkworm gut leaders. The gut was drawn through a series of decreasing-size holes in metal plates, reducing its diameter and producing a roughly uniform line. Each draw earned it another X. A 1X was the thickest; a 4X, the finest. Even today, a tippet's X-rating indicates its diameter, not its breaking strength; the same X-rating may have different strengths depending on the manufacturer (p. 163). Tippet material now comes as fine as 8X.

LEADER-CARE TIPS

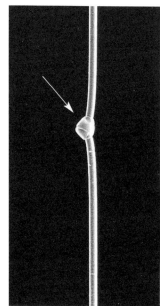

REPLACE your leader, or tippet section, if it develops a wind knot (arrow). These knots may reduce line strength by as much as 50 percent.

LEADER WALLETS protect leaders and tippet material from sunlight. You may want to label the individual sleeves for easy identification of leader type and diameter.

Clothing

The right apparel keeps you comfortable in any weather and makes you less visible to trout. Here's what to look for:

VESTS. A good vest should be lightweight, yet large enough to fit over a sweater or heavy shirt and hold your gear. One that feels bulky or heavy when empty will be tiring to wear when fully loaded. Some vests have an internal support strap to help distribute the weight of your gear evenly across your shoulders, and a padded collar to reduce the strain on your neck.

When choosing a vest, look for one with an assortment of pockets in various sizes for carrying accessories. The pockets should close securely with zippers or Velcro to keep small items from falling out.

The vest should also have a large zippered pocket in the back for storing lightweight rain gear; several rings for tying on small items, such as a squeeze bottle of floatant; and a ring at the back of the collar to hold a landing net.

Other handy features include a fly patch for drying flies before putting them in their box, and extended zipper tabs on the pockets, for easier opening with cold or gloved fingers.

If the weather is too warm for a vest or you only need to carry a small amount of gear, consider alternatives to a vest such as a chest or fanny pack, or a lightweight shirt with a number of oversize pockets.

A good chest pack should secure around your torso, as well as your neck, to keep the pack from swinging from side to side as you walk or wade.

HATS. Even on overcast days, you need a hat with a brim to reduce glare and make it easier to spot fish. Hats made especially for fly fishing often have a brim that is dark on the underside to further reduce glare.

The most popular type of hat is the baseball-style cap. Lightweight and comfortable, these caps come with visors of various lengths to shade your eyes. But they do not shade your ears and neck.

Some hats have a back flap that folds down to shade your neck and ears. A full-brim hat sheds rain and helps protect the back of your head from fly hooks. Avoid brightly colored hats, especially white ones, which could spook wary trout.

RAIN GEAR. It pays to carry an inexpensive plastic rain shell or poncho in your fishing vest. This way, you're prepared for an unexpected rain shower. If you know you'll be fishing in rainy conditions, wear more substantial rain gear.

A lightweight jacket made with a breathable material, such as Gore-Tex, can be worn all day without overheating. But some breathable materials are very expensive.

Traditional waxed or oiled cotton provides good protection, but it is expensive, weighs more than plastic or breathable rain gear and is too bulky to stash in your vest.

Although heavy and bulky, rubber rain gear provides the ultimate in rain protection. Worn over insulating layers, it will keep you dry and warm.

WADING JACKETS. A good wading jacket is your best bet for extended foul-weather fishing because it combines the waterproof qualities of a raincoat with the short length and large pockets of a vest. Some jackets include neoprene cuffs to keep out water and a drawstring hood designed to fit over most hats.

Accessories

You couldn't possibly carry every accessory and gadget sold at your fly shop – nor do you always need them. Your selection depends on the type of fishing you'll be doing. Following are the most common and useful items:

FLY BOXES. Important for storing, organizing and protecting your valuable flies, boxes come in many sizes and styles for different kinds of flies. A good fly box should be lightweight, hold your flies securely without crushing them, close tightly to keep out moisture and fit easily in a pocket of your fly vest. Popular fly-box styles include:

Compartment. This style is ideal for storing dry flies, which have delicate hackle that can crush easily. Some have compartments with individual, see-through lids that keep flies from blowing away or falling out when you open the box. Others have a single lid with movable dividers that let you adjust the size of the compartments to suit your flies. Be careful not to overfill the compartments; this will crush the flies.

Foam-lined. Inexpensive and lightweight, this style comes in flat and ripple foam, or a combination of the two. Flat foam is adequate for all but dry flies with delicate hackle. Ripple foam is better suited for dry flies. Hook them so the hackle falls in front of the ridges.

Clip. This classic style is used for storing wet flies, as well as streamers and nymphs. Most clip boxes are metal; as a result, they tend to be heavy and more expensive than other styles. Clips should never be used to hold dry flies.

Fleece. The traditional fleece-lined wallets are attractive but have little value for storing flies. The fleece will crush the feathers on almost any fly, and a fly put away damp will rust quickly.

Magnetic. Boxes with magnetic lining are gaining popularity, but tend to be heavier than other styles. They do not hold dry flies well because the hackle keeps the magnet from gripping the hook.

WEIGHTS. Several types of weights will help you get your fly down to the trout. These include:

Split Shot. By far the most common style, split shot comes in both lead and nontoxic lead substitute. Lead is softer and can be pinched securely to your leader without damaging it. Lead substitutes, such as tin, are lighter than similar-size lead shot and, because they are harder, are more likely to come off during a cast or damage your leader.

Moldable. Nontoxic tungsten compound is molded around your leader. You can easily adjust the weight, remove it and reuse it.

Twist-on. These narrow lead strips come in small spools or matchbook-style dispensers. When wrapped around a leader, they have a slim profile, making them snag-resistant. But they can damage your leader and create a "flat spot," which makes casting difficult.

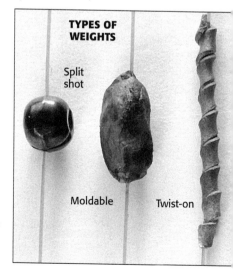

TYPES OF WEIGHTS

Split shot

Moldable

Twist-on

STRIKE INDICATORS. Once viewed with disdain by purists, strike indicators have nonetheless revolutionized nymph fishing. Indicators make it easier to tell when a fish has taken a subsurface fly. Today, most nymph fishermen add an indicator of some type to their leader, setting the hook at the slightest twitch or pause in the indicator's drift. Styles of indicators include:

Dry Fly. One of the oldest and most effective indicators is a dry fly; the wet fly or nymph is trailed below it on a length of tippet material, called a dropper. Because a fish can strike either fly, this style of indicator can increase your odds of success.

Yarn. A small tuft of poly yarn tied into a knot in your leader makes an inexpensive but highly effective indicator. Poly yarn floats well, comes in a variety of high-visibility colors and can be used to create a very large, yet light-weight, indicator.

Corky. This style is threaded onto the leader and held in place with a peg, usually the tip of a toothpick. A corky is simple to reposition, but in order to remove it, you must first snip off the fly.

Foam Adhesive. These popular peel-off indicators come in large sheets. The white or fluorescent tab is secured by folding it around the leader. These indicators float well and are easy to spot on the water, but often leave adhesive on your leader when removed, and are difficult to reposition.

Float Putty. Moldable, versatile and highly buoyant, float putty can be rolled into any size or shape, is easy to affix and is reusable, but can sometimes leave a residue on your leader.

Twist-on. These indicators are easy to add and remove, float well and are highly visible. Simply place your leader into the groove in the indicator and twist the flexible rubber ends. Twist-on indicators are easier to adjust than the adhesive style.

Fly Line. One of the simplest indicators is a section of floating fly line with the core removed. Thread the section onto your leader and secure it by pulling it over a knot. These indicators are ideal for slow water, or anywhere a larger indicator may spook the fish.

DRY-FLY FLOATANTS. Most dry flies only float for a short time before they absorb water and sink, losing their effectiveness. As a result, they must be treated with some type of floatant before use, and then periodically during use. Floatants come in paste, spray, powder and liquid forms (page 33).

Silicone dry-fly floatant can also be used to treat sections of leader and fly line to help them float higher.

FORCEPS. Also known as a hemostat, this medical tool is ideal for a variety of tasks, from removing small hooks to mashing down barbs. Flat-jaw forceps are better for mashing down barbs on tiny hooks than grooved-jaw. Most models lock closed, allowing you to clip them onto your vest.

ZINGER. This small, handy pin-on device contains a retractable cord that allows you to attach a variety of tools and gadgets to your vest.

THERMOMETER. Knowing the water temperature helps you predict insect and fish activity. In a typical trout stream, for instance, 52° water triggers many insect hatches. Select a small thermometer designed for use in water, preferably one with a protective case that can be attached to a zinger.

NIPPERS. Similar in design to nail clippers, nippers are essential for cutting line and trimming knots. They are sharper and cut more cleanly than ordinary clippers, making it easier to thread the tippet through the eye of a tiny fly. Some models have a needle for clearing head cement from hook eyes.

LEADER STRAIGHTENER. A coiled leader won't lie on the water properly. When it is drawn through a rubber leader straightener, the friction creates enough heat to straighten it.

MAGNIFIERS. Even anglers with good eyesight have trouble threading small hooks or tying fine tippet material. Clip-on magnifiers attach to the brim of your hat and flip up out of the way when not in use.

LIGHT. A small flashlight can extend your time on the water. Choose a clip-on model with a flexible neck that allows you to direct the beam and work with your hands free.

HOOK SHARPENER. A small ceramic, stone or diamond-dust hook sharpener is handy for putting a point on a small hook. You may need a file for larger hooks.

TAPE MEASURE. Choose a small retractable model that clips to your vest for measuring fish.

AMADOU. This highly absorbent natural tree fungus is useful for drawing the moisture out of a waterlogged fly. Amadou is particularly good for drying flies made from cul-de-canard (CDC) feathers, which come from the oil gland area of a duck and shouldn't be dressed with floatant.

LANDING NET. A net enables you to land your fish quickly; this way, they can be released with minimal stress.

A knotless, soft-nylon net with small mesh is crucial to prevent split fins and tails, which can cause infections.

Hang a short-handled net from the D-ring on the back collar of your vest using a French or magnetic clip.

SEINE. Use a small net to determine what insects trout might be feeding on below the water or on the surface.

SUNGLASSES. A good pair of polarized sunglasses greatly reduces glare and enables you to see trout below the surface, while protecting your eyes from errant flies. Side shields reduce glare even more. Be sure to buy glasses that block harmful UV rays.

BUG REPELLENT. Choose a solid-stick, roll-on or spray-on repellent that can be applied without getting it on your hands. Most bug repellents will quickly destroy a fly line.

LOG BOOK. Keeping a record of your fishing successes and failures can help improve your fishing. Use a log that allows you to record time, weather, location and hatch information, as well as flies used and fish caught.

MAPS. The back roads that lead to prime fishing waters usually do not appear on a standard highway map. Look for U.S. Geologic Survey quad maps, county maps or other maps with a high level of detail.

Store your maps in a clear, waterproof bag to protect them, and even if you have good maps, always carry a compass.

TYPES OF DRY-FLY FLOATANTS

1. LIQUID. These floatants, usually petroleum based, come in small jars. Simply dip your fly into the jar and allow it to dry completely before fishing. Liquid floatants dry more quickly than sprays and can be used on drowned flies. But the jars are quite heavy.

2. POWDER. If your fly becomes waterlogged or coated with fish slime, desiccant powders or crystals will remove the moisture, allowing you to treat it again with a paste or liquid. Choose a container that allows you to place the fly into the powder, close the lid and shake the bottle to coat the fly.

3. PASTE (left). The most popular type of floatant, pastes are easy to use and very effective. Most pastes are made of silicone, which, used sparingly, floats your fly high. But silicone pastes tend to get hard in cold weather, and using too much will gum up the hackle, wings and tail. It's best to squeeze a small amount of paste into the palm of your hand and rub it around with your finger until it becomes a liquid, then apply it to the fly.

4. SPRAY (right). Available in aerosol and pump, spray floatants are commonly used to treat new, unused flies. But sprays may take several hours to dry and do not work on flies that are already wet, making them impractical for use while fishing.

Wading Gear

Your choice of wading gear depends on the depth and temperature of the water you'll be in, how far you'll be walking and how much traction you'll need. Whatever gear you choose should fit well, keep you dry when wading and allow you to walk comfortably.

Wading gear comes in two common types: chest waders, which are best for wading in deep water; and hip boots, which are ideal for small, shallow streams or anywhere you are unlikely to wade deeper than mid-thigh.

Both types come in boot-foot and stocking-foot styles and are available in a variety of materials (opposite).

For warm weather, some anglers prefer wet wading. Instead of waders or hip boots, they wear shorts or lightweight, fast-drying pants, along with wading sandals (p. 36).

CHEST WADERS expand your fishing range by allowing you to wade deeper. Stocking-foot waders (left inset) require a separate wading boot, but are more comfortable to walk in than boot-foot waders (right inset), because they fit tighter and provide more ankle support. However, boot-foot waders are easier to put on and remove, and because they fit more loosely, won't restrict your circulation in cold water.

WADING GEAR MATERIALS

RUBBER (left) is inexpensive and durable, but can be heavy and baggy. Most rubber waders are not suited for wading in very warm or cold weather.

NYLON (right) is economical, lightweight and comfortable in hot weather. Wear fleece or wool pants for added insulation when you're wading in cold water.

BREATHABLE (left) materials, such as Gore-Tex, weigh about the same as nylon but are cooler in hot weather.

NEOPRENE (right) is warm, comfortable and durable, and it provides some flotation if you fall in. Neoprene wading gear is available in several thicknesses, ranging from 3mm to 5mm. It lets you move more easily than rubber or nylon, and fits tighter for less water resistance in swift current. But neoprene is more expensive than other materials and may be too warm in hot weather.

WADING SOLE TYPES

LUG SOLES offer good traction on muddy banks and streambeds. They are a poor choice, however, for slippery streambeds or fast water.

FELT SOLES provide good traction in most wading situations. They grip well on mossy rocks and in moderately fast water. Felt soles can be easily replaced if they wear out.

STUDDED SOLES provide maximum wading traction. They are ideal for swift or slippery-bottomed streams. The metal studs extend the life of the felt sole, as well. Strap-on cleats are also available.

WADING ACCESSORIES

WADING SANDALS with felt soles are designed to be worn on bare feet or with wool or polyester socks. Use them for wet wading in hot weather.

TIPS ON WADING

STAND sideways in swift current to minimize the force of the water and prevent your feet from being swept out from under you.

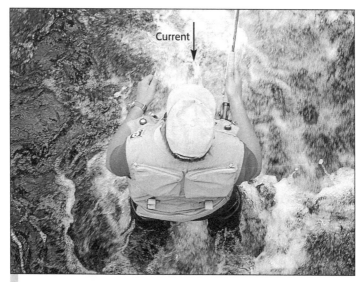

PIVOT upstream when turning around in fast water. If you pivot downstream, the current pushes you too fast.

2

BASIC FLY-FISHING
SKILLS

Fly-Fishing Knots

I n fly fishing, there can be as many as a dozen knots separating you and a hooked fish. Knowing which knots to choose and how to tie them can mean the difference between landing and losing that fish.

When tied incorrectly, monofilament line can cut through itself. An overhand knot, for instance, can reduce the strength of your leader by as much as 50 percent.

The knots that follow retain a high percentage of line strength when tied properly and are the best ones for the purposes described. For clarity, plain hooks rather than flies, and white line rather than mono, have been used in some of the knot sequences.

MOISTEN all knots before tightening. The friction caused by cinching a knot can heat the line and cause it to lose strength. Moistening your knots will reduce friction.

ATTACHING BACKING TO REEL

ARBOR KNOT. This simple knot will secure your backing so it won't slip around the spool or come off your reel if a trout takes out all your line.

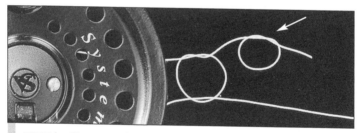

WRAP backing around spool, and then tie tag end of backing around standing line with overhand knot. Tie second overhand knot (arrow) in tag end.

TIGHTEN knot in tag end and then pull standing line until knot tightens securely against arbor. Keep pulling until knot in tag end snugs up against main knot.

ATTACHING FLY TO TIPPET

CLINCH KNOT. One of the most underrated fishing knots, the clinch knot is simple to tie, has excellent strength and can be easily undone with your fingernails. You must be careful, however, to make enough wraps so the knot won't pull out. The lighter the tippet, the more wraps you'll need. A 6X tippet may require as many as 8 wraps; a very heavy tippet, only 3½.

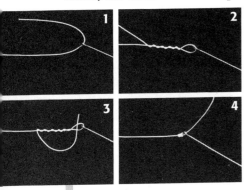

(1)PASS end of tippet through hook eye. (2)WIND tag end around standing line 3½ to 8 times, depending on tippet diameter. (3)BRING tag end back through loop nearest hook eye. (4)PULL standing line until knot is snug against hook eye. Trim tag.

DUNCAN LOOP (OR UNI-KNOT). Among the strongest knots for attaching a fly, the Duncan loop can be snugged up with the loop open to allow the fly to swing freely, or pulled tight against the hook. The loop may close from the pull of a fish, an advantage in absorbing the shock of a hook set, but you can easily reopen it by carefully sliding the knot back.

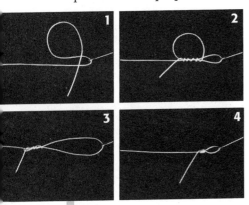

(1)PASS end of tippet through hook. Form loop in tag end, as shown. (2)PASS tag end through loop. Wind tag end through loop and around standing line 4 times, winding away from hook. (3)PULL tag end to snug up knot. (4)SLIDE knot to desired position by pulling on standing line. Trim tag.

MAKING A LOOP IN A LEADER

DOUBLE SURGEON'S LOOP. This is the simplest knot for making a loop in either end of a leader. The loop can then be attached to a loop in the fly line or to another leader section with a loop-to-loop connection (p. 47).

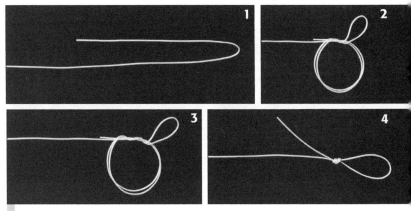

(1)DOUBLE UP the last 6 inches of the leader. (2)MAKE a loose over-hand knot in double line. (3)PASS loop end through knot a second time to form double overhand knot. (4)TIGHTEN by holding loop while pulling standing line and tag end until snug. Trim tag closely.

PERFECTION LOOP. Although the perfection loop is more diffi-cult to tie than a surgeon's loop and takes a little more time to learn, it forms a more compact knot that is equally strong.

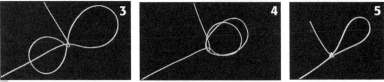

(1)FORM a loop in leader by passing tag end behind standing line, tag facing right. (2)FORM a second loop in front of first by passing tag end around and then behind first loop. (3)PASS tag end between first two loops; hold tag end to left side. (4)PULL second loop through first loop from behind. TIGHTEN knot by pulling on loop and standing line. Tag should be at right angle to standing line. Trim tag closely.

JOINING TWO SECTIONS OF MONOFILAMENT

DOUBLE SURGEON'S KNOT. This knot is best for join-ing sections of leader or tippet material that differ by more than .003 inch in diameter. It is easier to tie and stronger than a blood knot, but does not lay out perfectly straight.

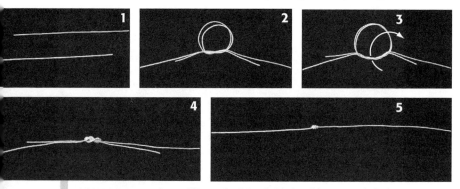

(1)PLACE two sections of line to be joined side by side, tag ends facing opposite directions. (2)MAKE a loop in double line. Pass both ends of line on right through loop to form an overhand knot. (3)PASS same ends through loop a second time to form double overhand knot. (4)TIGHTEN knot by pulling all four ends slowly and evenly. (5)TRIM tag ends close to knot.

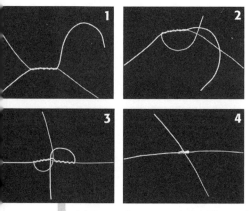

BLOOD KNOT. This knot is a good choice for joining two sections of similar-diameter leader or tippet material. It works better than a double sur-geon's knot for joining long sections of mono, and forms a connection that lays out straighter.

(1)CROSS the two sections of line to be joined, and then wrap one tag end around standing part of other line 5 to 7 times, depending on line diameter. (2)PASS tag end back between the two lines. (3)WRAP other tag end around other standing line 5 to 7 times. (4)PULL standing lines to tighten knot. Trim tags closely.

JOINING FLY LINE TO BACKING OR LEADER

ALBRIGHT KNOT. The Albright knot is easier to tie than the tube knot, but is bulkier because the fly line is doubled. Albright knots are used primarily for attaching the backing to the fly line.

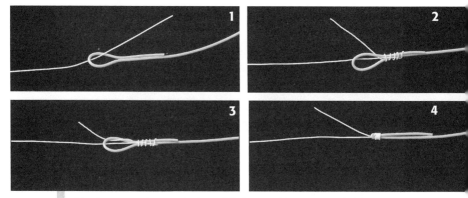

(1) DOUBLE UP last two inches of fly line and pass tag end of backing or leader butt through the loop. (2) WIND backing or leader butt over itself and doubled fly line 5 to 8 times, depending on line diameter. (3) PASS backing or leader butt through loop so it comes out on the same side it entered. (4) TIGHTEN by slowly pulling on all four lines. Pull until knot is tight; trim ends closely.

TUBE KNOT. Because the tube knot is not as bulky as the Albright knot, it is a better choice for attaching the butt section of a fly leader or a permanent butt section to a fly line.

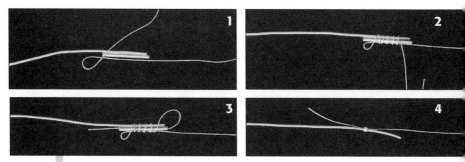

(1) PLACE hollow tube alongside fly line, and loop butt end of leader alongside tube, as shown. (2) WRAP butt end around tube, fly line and standing part of leader 5 to 6 times. (3) PASS butt through tube as shown. Carefully remove tube. Pull tag end and standing part of leader until knot is just snug. (4) TIGHTEN knot slowly, using fingernails to position wraps evenly before tightening completely. Closely trim tag ends.

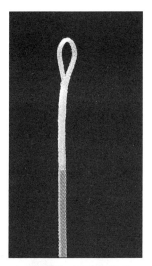

MAKING A LOOP IN YOUR FLY LINE

BRAIDED-LOOP CONNECTOR. A braided-loop connector slips over the end of your fly line. Then, you can easily attach your leader using a loop-to-loop connection (opposite). Be sure to buy a connector that matches the size of your fly line.

Although braided-loop connectors are handy, some experts believe they hinge too much on the cast, so the leader does not roll over properly.

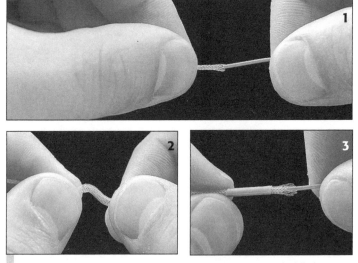

(1)SQUEEZE end of connector to open braids; insert end of fly line.(2) WORK fly line into connector by alternately squeezing the braids and pushing on the line. Continue until line is as far into connector as possible; it must be in at least 2 inches to be secure. (3) SLIDE plastic sleeve that comes with connector down to cover the braided end, which may be frayed. DAB Super Glue on the connector, if desired. Because the connector operates on the "Chinese finger trap" principle, however, this step is usually unnecessary.

LOOP-TO-LOOP CONNECTION. Use the loop-to-loop connection for joining several leader sections or attaching your leader to a braided-loop connector (p. 46). This way, you can change leaders or leader sections quickly and easily.

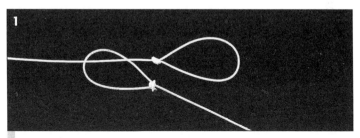

PASS loop in first section through loop in second section.

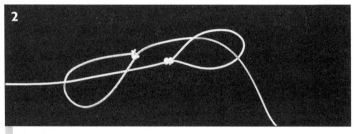

THREAD other end of second section through loop in first section.

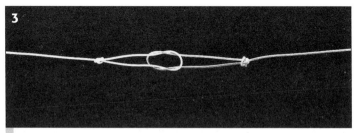

PULL standing parts of both sections until knot snugs up.

Fly Casting

T he skill of accurately casting a weightless fly forms the foundation of fly fishing. Because the fly must land delicately without alarming the trout and give the illusion of life, a good cast can be the factor in fooling the fish into taking your fly.

In fly fishing, the line, rather than the lure, provides the necessary casting weight. The line, in turn, propels the leader and fly to your target.

Smooth, accurate fly casting comes with time and practice. Before you attempt to fish, practice the basic overhead cast pp. 52-53) until you are comfortably throwing line 25 to 40 feet – the distance at which most fish are caught.

In the past, most fly-casting instruction was based on the clock-face method, with the fly rod representing the hour hand of an imaginary clock and the casting motion performed overhead between the 10- and 2-o'clock positions. This technique worked fine for short to medium casts, but made learning to cast longer distances difficult.

Separating the casting motion into its individual parts helps you understand the mechanics of a cast, so you can cast more effectively. How you execute the elements of a cast is more important than where on the face of a clock.

Once you have mastered the basic elements, apply them to perfect the overhead cast and then to practice false casting, distance casting and roll casting.

TIPS FOR PRACTICING FLY CASTING

No one becomes an expert fly caster overnight. It may take years of practice to perfect the skill of placing the fly precisely where you want it under various conditions. But fly casting is hardly a chore; many fly fishermen spend hours practicing just for the pleasure of throwing a fly line. Before attempting to fish, practice casting over grass to a fixed target (below). Never use a fly on the end of your leader when practicing on grass.

CHOOSE a practice surface of water or grass with no trees nearby to interfere with your line. Avoid casting over surfaces such as gravel or asphalt, which can damage your line.

TIE a piece of fluorescent yarn to the end of your leader in place of a fly. The yarn won't snag, is safer than a sharp hook and helps you see the end of your leader in the air and on the ground.

PRACTICE accuracy, which is usually more important than distance. Use a paper plate or plastic hoop as a casting target. Position targets at various distances and practice placing the end of your leader onto each target.

THE ELEMENTS OF A CASTING STROKE

ACCELERATE gradually and continuously throughout this phase of the casting stroke. This gradual application of speed helps you begin to focus the energy of the cast in the direction you want the line to go.

APPLY a short burst of speed at the end of the acceleration phase to bend, or load, the rod. The shorter the speed stroke, the tighter the loop will be.

STOP the rod suddenly at the end of the short speed stroke, causing the rod to straighten, or unload, quickly. This transfers the energy from the rod to the line, forming a tight loop and propelling the line. Even with a poor acceleration and speed stroke, stopping the rod crisply will form a tight loop and cause the line to unroll smoothly. Many beginning fly casters fail to stop the rod quickly enough, resulting in poor loops.

THE CASTING PLANE

The casting plane is the path of the rod tip, and thus the line, as it travels back and forth in the air. Although commonly called a "plane," the casting plane is really just an imaginary line.

But to give you the tightest loops and most efficient casts, this line must be as straight as possible. In other words, the path of the forward cast should be in line with that of the backcast. To accomplish this, your forearm and wrist should also be moving on a straight path, not pivoting at the elbow. Picture the motion that would be needed to pound nails in opposite sides of a door frame with a two-headed hammer, and use this same straight back-and-forth motion in your casts. If your forearm and rod tip travel in an arc, rather than a straight line, your casting loop will open up.

The casting plane is not always parallel to the ground. In situations where there is an obstruction behind you, tilt your casting plane forward to lift your backcast above it (right).

When casting sidearm to avoid overhead obstructions, such as overhanging limbs, or to keep from spooking fish in clear water, many anglers find it more difficult to maintain a straight casting plane, because their wrist and elbow tend to pivot. But the

TILT the casting plane forward to raise your backcast when there is a high bank or brush behind you.

path of the line is just as important for maintaining tight loops in sidearm casting as it is in overhead casting. Watch the path of your line as you cast until you develop a feel for the arm motion needed to achieve a straight casting plane.

THE OVERHEAD CAST

The overhead cast is used to pick up the fly line and lay it back down in order to reposition the line, leader and fly on the water. This basic and essential cast forms the foundation of many other fly-fishing casts. A fly angler may perform this cast dozens of times in a single hour of fishing.

Use the overhead cast for short to middistance casting.

BEGIN by letting out the desired amount of fly line in front of you. Stand facing your target with your feet spread comfortably apart. Position your rod hand so the tip of the rod is pointing in the direction of your target, with your rod, forearm and wrist aligned. Lower your rod tip and remove the slack from the line.

RAISE your rod and begin to accelerate slowly and continuously, until entire fly line is off the water.

APPLY a short backward speed stroke, forcing a bend in the rod and generating the energy necessary to propel the line into the backcast.

STOP the rod crisply. A loop will form in the line as it moves overhead. The shorter the speed stroke and straighter the casting plane, the tighter the loop will be.

PAUSE as the backcast unrolls behind you. When the line unrolls to only a small "J" in the air, begin your forward acceleration.

APPLY a short forward speed stroke and immediately stop the rod (shown). Aim your cast about eye level above your target. Let the line settle to the water, while lowering the rod tip to the fishing position.

THE FALSE CAST

The false cast begins the same as the overhead cast, with a simple backcast and forward cast. But the false cast differs from the overhead in that the line is not allowed to settle to the water following the forward cast. Instead, as your line begins to straighten in front, you make another backcast. You can repeat this back-and-forth motion several times, if necessary, depending on the purpose of the cast. The false cast is used mainly to change direction between casts, gauge the distance of your cast and let out fly line (below). It can also be used to cancel an off-target cast or dry a waterlogged fly in the air.

Timing is important. Many fly fishermen hurry their forward casts, so they often "crack the whip" with the line, possibly breaking off the fly. When learning, turn your head and watch your backcast unroll behind you. When the line unrolls to a small "J," begin your forward cast.

Aim your forward cast higher than you would on an overhead cast. Remember that the fly line will travel in the direction that your rod tip was moving when you stopped the rod. Aiming your rod higher on the forward cast will give the line more time to unroll and allow you to begin your backcast without the line falling to the water.

The acceleration, speed stroke and stop are important. So is the casting plane. Keep the rod tip traveling in a straight line parallel to the desired path of the fly line. The forward cast should be on the same plane as the backcast. Keep your wrist as straight as possible when false casting; bending it will open your casting loops.

HOW TO LET OUT LINE WITH A FALSE CAST

STRIP *several feet of fly line from the reel. As your forward cast unrolls in the air, let a small amount of line slip through your fingers (shown). Let out only a little at a time or you will throw slack into the line, making it difficult to load the rod on the next stroke. Repeat until you have let out the desired amount of line.*

HOW TO FALSE CAST

LIFT the line off the water as you would on a normal overhead cast.

LET the backcast unroll behind you until the line forms a small "J." Then begin your forward cast.

AIM your forward cast higher than you would on an overhead cast. Do not allow the line to settle to the water. Instead, wait until the small "J" forms in the line and begin another backcast. Repeat as necessary.

THE DISTANCE CAST

Most beginning fly casters learn to make short casts fairly quickly. But distance casting is more complicated and difficult to learn. Here are some techniques to help your distance casting.

Shooting line. This method involves making several false casts, then letting out the desired amount of line on the final forward cast (below). For hard-to-reach fish, you should learn to shoot line at least 30 feet.

Longer rod drift. Lengthening your casting strokes gives you the extra momentum needed for longer casts. The word "drift" is somewhat misleading; it simply refers to the length of these strokes, which depends on the length of the cast. Use longer rod drift, combined with the double haul, for casting even greater distances.

The double haul. This technique involves making a short tug, or haul, on the line during the acceleration phase on both the forward and backcast (opposite). This loads the rod more quickly, increasing line speed. Besides giving you more distance, the double haul also helps you punch the line into the wind.

HOW TO SHOOT LINE

FORM an "O" with the fingers of your line hand after you've stopped the rod. Let the forward cast pull the loose line through your fingers; the "O" will help feed the line through the stripping guide without bunching up.

HOW TO MAKE A DOUBLE HAUL

(1)MAKE a short, smooth downward haul, about 4 to 6 inches long, during the acceleration phase of the backcast. (2)BRING your line hand back up immediately after the haul. Let the line unroll behind you as you would on a normal overhead cast.

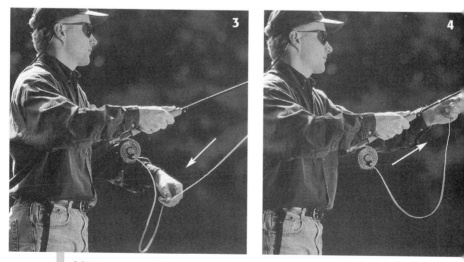

(3)MAKE a second haul, equal in length to the first, during the acceleration phase of the forward cast. (4)BRING your line hand back up again immediately after the haul. If you are shooting line, form an "O" with your line hand instead.

THE ROLL CAST

Occasionally, you'll find yourself in a situation where obstacles, such as streamside vegetation or a high bank, leave you no room for a backcast. The roll cast allows you to cast line forward without a backcast, and lets you get into tight places where you wouldn't dare risk a backcast.

Because you've eliminated the backcast, you must instead load the rod by using the friction of the water on the line (below). You'll need to practice this cast on the water, because grass does not provide enough friction.

Double-taper lines are easier to roll cast than weight-forward lines. The consistent diameter of the long belly transfers energy smoothly, so the line rolls out more easily.

HOW TO ROLL CAST

(1) LIFT your rod tip slowly until it is slightly behind you and the line is on the water in front of you. Pause momentarily until the line stops moving toward you. This pause lets the water "grip" the line, creating enough friction to load the rod. (2) ACCELERATE steadily, make a short speed stroke, then stop the rod quickly. (3) LET the fly line roll out in front of you; it should form an elliptical loop and straighten out before settling to the water.

RETRIEVING LINE

How you take in line is as important as how you cast it out. A proper retrieve can give your fly action and let you control the line as you take it in, eliminating slack for easier strike detection and quicker hook sets.

The hand retrieve lets you take in line slowly and steadily, and gives you great sensitivity to strikes. It works well for fishing dry flies and nymphs in slow water.

HOW TO MAKE A HAND-TWIST RETRIEVE

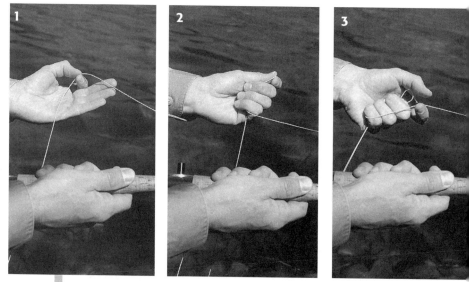

(1) PINCH line between thumb and index finger of line hand. Reach out with other three fingers to begin taking in line. (2) GRASP line with these three fingers and pinch line against palm of hand. Release line from between thumb and index finger. (3) REPEAT as necessary. Hold recovered line in palm, if desired, or allow it to fall to water as you continue to take in line.

MENDING LINE

When you cast a fly across a current to slower water, the swifter current catches your line and forms a downstream bow. If left unchecked, this bow will pull the fly downstream faster than the current it's in, causing an unnatural wake. This phenomenon is called drag. Drag can spook a wary trout and put it down for some time. The way to combat this problem is to mend the line, adjusting its position to eliminate drag.

THE UPSTREAM MEND

(1)STRIP several feet of line from your reel. Allow your fly to drift downstream until just before the bow in the line causes the fly to drag. (2)FLIP the line upstream with a short, semicircular motion of the rod tip (arrow). Let the slack line slip through your fingers as you mend, to prevent disturbing the fly. The line should settle to the water with an upstream bow. Repeat as necessary.

THE DOWNSTREAM MEND

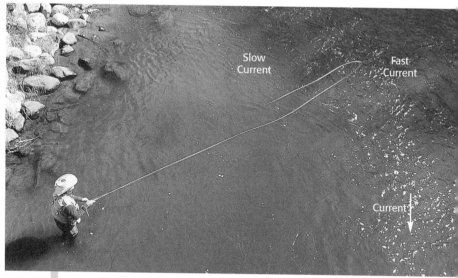

MAKE a cast; let the line settle to the water. The fast current will take the end of the line downstream, while the rest of the line will form an upstream bow in the slow current. Allow the line to drift until just before the fly begins to drag.

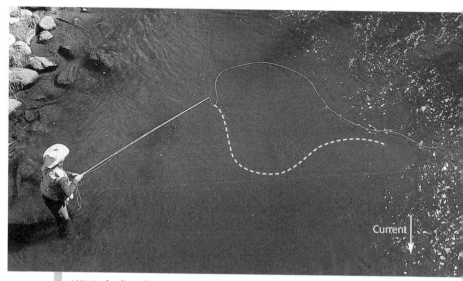

MEND the line downstream (dotted line) with a short, semicircular motion of the rod tip. Let out a small amount of slack line with each mend to avoid disturbing the fly.

3
TROUT & THEIR
ENVIRONMENT

Trout Basics

Trout have long been considered superior gamefish, the ultimate in wariness and fighting ability. In years past, many anglers regarded them as the only true gamefish.

Unfortunately, this wary nature has led to the popular notion that the fish are superintelligent, and therefore extremely difficult for the average angler to catch. But there is no evidence to indicate they are more intelligent than other gamefish species.

The notion is reinforced when anglers see feeding trout being "put down" by even the slightest movement or vibration. But this instinctive reaction should not be confused with intelligence. Like any other fish, trout become conditioned to flee for cover to avoid predators. As soon as they hatch, trout face attacks from predatory insects, crayfish and small fish. As they grow older, they are attacked by larger fish and by kingfishers, herons and other predatory birds. Most stream fishermen have seen dead trout along the bank with gaping beak wounds in their heads. The wariness of trout also results from natural selection; those that lack wariness do not live to reproduce.

The main thing that distinguishes trout from many other gamefish is their preference for cold water. Although temperature preferences vary among trout, most need water temperatures from 50° to 65°F, and avoid temperatures above 70°. This requirement means they live only in streams or lakes fed by springs or snow melt, or in lakes with plenty of cold, well-oxygenated water in the depths.

Trout belong to the family Salmonidae and are referred to as salmonids. Besides trout, the family includes salmon, grayling (mainly in Alaska, the Yukon and the Northwest Territories) and whitefish, which are widely distributed in the northern states and Canada but are of only minor importance to anglers.

Powerful fighters, trout have remarkable stamina. Some species, like rainbow trout, leap repeatedly when hooked; others, like brook trout, wage a deep, bulldog-style battle.

Although salmonids are excellent eating, the trend is toward catch-and-release fishing. In some heavily fished waters, catch-and-release is mandatory. This practice ensures that the fish remain in a stream long enough to spawn and produce "wild" progeny. The other alternative, frowned upon by most trout enthusiasts, is put-and-take stocking.

Senses

THE INNER EAR detects high-frequency vibrations and helps in maintaining balance.

NARES are used to smell odors, avoid predators, locate spawning areas and find food.

EYES are the trout's primary defense against predators and are also used to locate food and to feed.

Experienced fly fishermen know, from many long days spent on the water, that trout have extremely acute senses. The approach and presentation must be very good if you're to have any chance at catching trout. A presentation marred by a sudden movement, a shadow or glint of light off your equipment, or even a heavy footstep, will send a trout into deep cover. Although it has a keen sense of smell and a well-developed lateral line sense (p. 70), it is the trout's vision that makes it one of the most challenging of all gamefish.

VISION. Like other predatory fish, trout rely primarily on their vision to detect danger and find food. Among fishermen, trout have a reputation for possessing extremely acute eyesight, but it has not been established that the trout's vision is more highly developed than that of other species. Its reputation may be due to the simple fact that trout typically live in very clear, shallow water, where visibility is excellent.

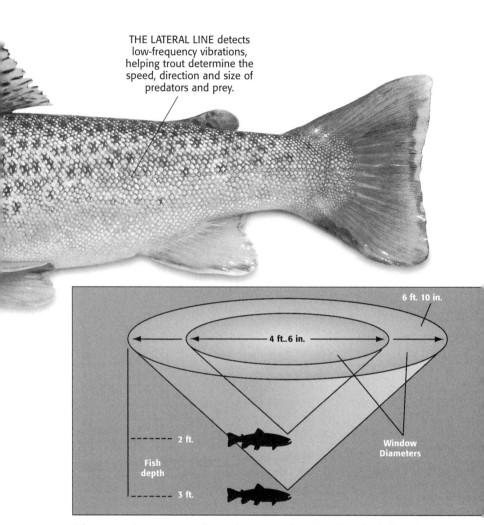

THE LATERAL LINE detects low-frequency vibrations, helping trout determine the speed, direction and size of predators and prey.

6 ft. 10 in.

4 ft..6 in.

2 ft.

Fish depth

3 ft.

Window Diameters

The trout has a cone-shaped range of vision that is defined by a circular window, called the Snell circle, on the surface of the water. The circle's diameter is about twice as wide as the fish is deep. At a depth of two feet, for example, the Snell circle is roughly four feet in diameter; at four feet of depth, the circle of vision is about eight feet in diameter. Outside this cone the fish sees nothing above the water, and the surface from below appears black, or like a mirror.

The trout's field of vision is larger than you would expect, due to the scientific principle of light refraction. The principle states that light rays passing from air to water are bent, or refracted, by an amount that depends upon the angle at which the light rays are striking the surface of the water. When fishing for trout, then, you must remember that the trout's peripheral vision around the perimeter of the Snell circle extends quite low to the horizon. If you stay very low – less than 10° up from the water at the edge of the fish's window of vision – the trout may not see you at all as you approach and cast your fly. In addition, images on the edge of the Snell circle appear quite distorted because they are severely refracted. By staying low, you improve the chance that

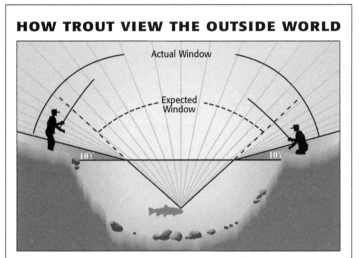

HOW TROUT VIEW THE OUTSIDE WORLD

LIGHT RAYS entering the water vertically are not bent at all, so trout clearly see objects directly above them. Rays entering the water at an angle are bent; the lower the angle, the more the distortion. Because of this bending, the actual window of view is much wider than the expected window. Although both anglers in this diagram are out of the expected window, the trout can still see them. The angler on the left, however, is more clearly visible than the one on the right, because the light rays reflecting off him into the water are not bent as much. To get completely out of the trout's window, you would have to stay in the purple zone, at an angle of about 10° above the water's surface. If you're 40 feet from the edge of the window, you can stand up without being seen; at 20 feet, you would have to kneel.

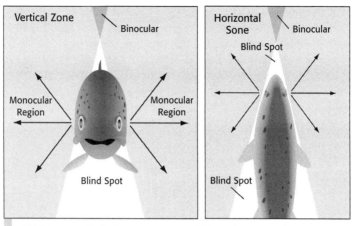

VISION zones include narrow areas of binocular vision above and in front of the fish, wide zones of monocular sight to the sides, and blind spots below and behind the fish. Trout usually strike at food that lies in the binocular zone.

the trout won't recognize you as a predator, even if it does detect your shape.

Although the trout's daytime vision is very acute, the story is different at night. Because their night vision is at best only fair, most trout do very little feeding after dark. The exception is large brown trout, which are vulnerable at night to flies that produce noise or vibration.

The trout's eyes are positioned on the side of the head, which gives it a wide field of vision but also creates some blind spots (above). Trout have both binocular vision and monocular vision. In the horizontal plane, the binocular field, in which the fish can focus with both eyes, is between 30° and 36° wide, depending on the species. The monocular field, where the fish can see with only one eye, is 150° on both sides of the head, which leaves a blind spot of roughly 30° directly behind the fish.

In the vertical plane, trout have a narrow range of binocular vision above the head, wide ranges of monocular vision to the sides, and a significant blind spot below.

As most fly fishermen know, a trout is most likely to spot and strike a fly that appears in its binocular zone above and straight ahead, where the fish can best perceive depth and detail. This is also the most efficient feeding zone for the trout, since it can rise to feed and drop back down into its resting lie with a minimal expenditure of energy. If a fly is spotted to the side in the monocular zone, the trout must spend more energy to reach the target. If it chooses to attack such a target, a trout will almost always line itself up so the fly lies in the binocular field before striking.

Trout have relatively good color perception, especially in shallow, clear water. Like humans, trout see brightness and color by means of tiny receptors, called rods and cones, in the retinas of the eyes. However, the trout's color perception is greatly affected by the hue of the water and by the color of the above-water background. It's rarely necessary for your imitation to match the exact color of the food it mimics. The general color tone seems to be more important than hue. For example, if trout are actively feeding on light-toned brown insects, they are more likely to respond to a light gray imitation than to a dark brown fly.

SMELL. Trout have a very well developed sense of smell, which can detect odors in concentrations of just a few parts per million. Water is drawn into the front opening, or nare, passes through the nasal sac inside the snout, and is expelled out through the back nare. Smell is used to avoid predators, locate spawning areas, and to find food.

Research has shown that some species of the trout family can sense a chemical called L-serine, which is emitted by bears as well as by humans, and will avoid waters containing this substance.

Trout sometimes use smell to identify edible food. This ability is often used when trout are feeding underwater on slow-moving targets, but is less important when the fish are feeding on foods that are rapidly moving across the surface of the water. When surface feeding, vision and lateral-line sense enable trout to locate prey almost instantly.

Though the trout's sense of smell is more important when fishing the subsurface, it is still a consideration for the surface angler. Always try to avoid any unnatural odors on your flies and wading gear.

LATERAL LINE. The lateral-line system is a network of ultrasensitive nerve endings found along the side of the

THE LATERAL LINE and the INNER EAR allow trout to detect movements and disturbances in their environment. An angler must use care if he wants to approach close enough to successfully present a fly. Anglers often spook catchable fish without ever knowing they were there. Careful wading is one key element to approaching close enough to catch fish.

trout's body. The lateral line senses low-frequency vibrations of objects in the water that are near but not touching the fish. Using lateral-line sense, trout can determine the speed, direction of movement, and size of predators and prey moving through the water. In dirty waters, the lateral line can be even more important than sight when the fish is feeding.

When wading the stream or walking the bank, an experienced fly fisherman steps very carefully to avoid making noises that can spook the fish. Kicking an underwater stone or tromping with heavy footsteps on the adjacent riverbank may be all it takes to scare away or alert every trout in the immediate neighborhood.

HEARING. Fish hear sound with a different sensory system than they use to detect vibrations. Although they don't have external ears – which are not needed because sound travels well through water – trout do have an inner ear that functions much the same way as human ears. Tiny bones and semicircular canals in the inner ear preceive high-frequency vibrations or waves. The inner ear also helps the fish maintain its balance in the current.

The Rise

When a trout takes a floating insect, the surface disturbance is called a rise. Observing a rise can tell you not only where the fish is located, but also what it's eating. Inexperienced fishermen often make the mistake of casting directly to a rise in hopes of catching the trout. But in most cases, the rise occurs well downstream of the trout's lie.

If you cast straight to the rise, your fly will likely fall in the trout's blind spot and will be ignored. In most cases, the best presentation is to deliver the fly slightly upstream of the rise, preferably within the trout's zone of binocular vision.

In very slow currents, however, trout sometimes continue to travel forward rather than return to a holding lie after each rise. When you see a trout behaving this way, try to anticipate where the fish will travel next and cast to that spot. Don't cast too close to the last rise when trout are in this kind of feeding pattern, because you have a good chance of spooking the fish. If you lead the fish too much, on the other hand, you'll usually be able to recast.

Rises can be categorized according to the foods the fish are eating and by the types of water they are feeding in. By carefully observing how trout are rising, you may be able to determine the type of insect being eaten, and maybe even its life stage. This information can help you create a winning strategy for catching the trout. The photos on pages 74-75 show how to identify and interpret some of the most common rise forms.

HOLD (left). The trout faces into the current when feeding, watching the surface directly ahead to spot insects and other food items drifting into the window of vision. DRIFT (right). After spotting an insect, the trout begins to drift downstream, examining the potential meal while adjusting its fins to rise to the surface. The drift may be very short, or as long as 25 feet, depending on the speed of the current and the nourishment value of the food.

RISE (left). The trout disturbs the surface as it takes the insect, creating a splash or dimpling the water with a noticeable ring. If you see bubbles left behind, it's a good indication that the food was taken on the surface rather than just below it – when inhaling a fly on the surface, trout often take in air, which they expel through their gills. RETURN (right). The trout returns upstream to its lie immediately after the rise. The distance between the rise and the lie depends on the water depth and current speed. In waters 3 feet deep or less, a dry fly delivered to a spot 3 to 4 feet up-current from the rise will drift directly over the trout's lie.

COMMON RISE FORMS

SIPPING RISE. This type of subtle rise generally indicates that fish are leisurely feeding on flies resting on the surface of the water. As the trout sucks in an insect, it creates a series of concentric rings. Sipping rises are difficult to spot in rough water. Trout feeding in sips are vulnerable to an adult fly imitation cast well ahead of the rise, provided the fly resembles the actual insects being eaten.

HEAD-AND-TAIL RISE. This rise usually means the trout is feeding on insects stuck in the surface film. The trout's head appears first; then the dorsal fin and tail are visible as the fish rolls. An angler often gets results by presenting a fly that resembles a terrestrial, an emerging aquatic insect or a spent adult insect. The best presentation is to cast the fly up-current from the trout's last rise and let it drift naturally past the lie.

TAILING. Fishermen often mistake a "tailing" fish for a feeding rise. In all likelihood, these fish are rooting for immature insects or other foods from the bottom of the stream. Trout behaving this way aren't likely to take a dry fly; you should fish using subsurface techniques instead.

Trout Stream Habitat

Mention the term "trout stream," and most people think of flowing water that is cold, clear and unpolluted. This stereotype is accurate, but there are other requirements as well. The quantity and size of trout a stream produces depend on the factors discussed on the following pages.

WATER FERTILITY

A stream's fertility, or level of dissolved minerals, affects the production of plankton, the fundamental link in the aquatic food chain. Fertility depends mainly on the water source. Limestone streams generally have a considerably higher mineral content than freestone streams.

A limestone stream is normally fed by underground springs rich in calcium carbonate, an important nutrient, and flows over a streambed that supplies even more minerals. Limestone streams have more aquatic vegetation, produce more insects and crustaceans, and generally grow more and larger trout.

A freestone stream is fed by runoff or springs with a low mineral content. It typically flows over a streambed that contributes few nutrients to the water. The most productive freestone streams pick up extra nutrients from fertile tributaries. For more details on stream types, see page 83.

All streams that support permanent trout populations have one thing in common: a reliable source of cold water. The cold water usually comes from springs or meltwater from snow or glaciers, but in heavily forested areas it may come from water that seeps out of the soil. Streams fed by ordinary surface runoff become too warm for trout in midsummer, except in the North or at high altitudes, where air temperatures stay cool all year.

Some trout can survive at surprisingly warm water temperatures. Browns and rainbows, for instance, live in streams where temperatures sometimes rise into the low 80s.

Headwaters

Middle zone

HEADWATERS. The headwaters serves as a spawning and rearing area, but may be too small to support large trout. Because of the cold water, headwaters are best suited to brook trout.

MIDDLE ZONE. The middle zone has cool water and is the most productive part of the stream. It has the best insect crop and generally supports the highest population of adult trout, often brooks, browns and rainbows.

But at these temperatures, they usually feed very little, their growth rate slows, and their resistance to disease diminishes.

The stream temperature depends not only on the water source, but also on the shape and gradient of the channel, and the amount of shade provided by streamside vegetation (pp. 80-81). Streams with a distinct cold-water source commonly have the temperature zones described below.

Key to Temperature Zones

Cold Water	Cool Water	Warm Water
(below 55°)	(55-70°)	(above 70°)

Key to Trout Species

Brook Trout	Rainbow Trout	Brown Trout

Lower zone

LOWER ZONE. The water is warm, the current slow and the bottom silty. The lower zone supports few trout, but may hold some of the largest ones. You may find big browns along with suckers, carp and catfish.

Gradient, Current Speed & Bottom Type

Besides affecting water temperature, the gradient, or slope, of the streambed also influences current speed and bottom composition. The higher the gradient, the faster the current and the larger the particles that the current will carry.

Medium gradient (left) – moderate current, gravel-rubble bottom. Low gradient (right) – slow current, sand-silt bottom.

The most productive trout streams have a medium gradient, ranging from .5 to 2 percent, which converts to a drop of 25 to 100 feet per stream mile. Such a stream usually has moderate current and a gravel-rubble bottom, which produces abundant insect life and provides a good spawning substrate.

Mountain streams may have a much higher gradient, sometimes as great as 15 percent. Above 7 percent, a stream must have stairstep pools, pocket water (p. 91), log jams or other slack-water areas if it is to support trout. Without these features, the current is too swift.

If a stream has a gradient of less than .5 percent, the water is likely to be too warm for trout and the current may not be strong enough to wash away silt that enters the stream from nearby farm fields, logging operations and overgrazed or otherwise eroded streambanks. Silt fills the spaces between the gravel, destroying insect habitat and causing eggs deposited in the gravel to suffocate. Conservation agencies attempt to reduce siltation by fencing trout streams to keep out cattle, thereby allowing streambank vegetation to redevelop.

SHAPE OF STREAM CHANNEL

The shape of the stream channel affects a stream's water temperature, current speed and habitat diversity. A narrow, deep channel is generally best. In a wide, shallow one, a higher percentage of the water is exposed to the air and sun, causing the water to warm more rapidly.

Where the channel is too wide, there is not enough current to keep silt in suspension. As it settles out, the silt smothers gravel beds that provide food and spawning habitat. Stream-improvement projects are often intended to narrow a channel that has been widened by eroding banks or beaver dams.

Streams that meander have more diverse habitat than streams with a straight channel and, consequently, have more natural cover for trout. As a stream winds along, banks along the outside bends become undercut and tree roots wash out, making ideal hiding spots. Where habitat is varied, so is the food supply. Many types of aquatic insects thrive in riffles and runs; baitfish and burrowing aquatic insects abound in pools. If a stream has aquatic vegetation, like stonewort or watercress, the plants often host scuds, midge larvae and other trout foods. Diverse habitat also provides plenty of resting and spawning areas.

When the channel is artificially straightened, riffle-run-pool habitat disappears, and so do the trout.

MEANDERING streams (left) have diverse trout habitat; channelized streams (right), uniform habitat.

81

STABILITY OF FLOW

Almost any stream can support trout in spring, when water temperatures are cool and flows are high. But trout must live in the stream year-round. If the flow falls too low, even for a few days, trout will probably not survive.

Low flows present the biggest problem in late summer, especially in areas with little forest cover to preserve ground moisture. If the weather is hot and there has been little rain, too much water evaporates from the stream, reducing the depth and slowing the current so the remaining water warms faster. Even if trout survive the warm water, they suffer so much stress that they may not feed.

Low water can also be a problem in winter. In a dry year, winter flows may drop so low that the stream freezes to the bottom.

Streams fed by large underground springs are the most stable. Springs ensure at least a minimal flow that prevents the stream from drying up during a drought. And because spring water comes out of the ground at the same temperature year-round, these streams stay cool in summer and relatively warm in winter.

CLARITY, DISSOLVED OXYGEN & PH

Most trout species prefer clear water, although some, like browns and rainbows, can tolerate low clarity. Clear water allows sunlight to penetrate to the streambed, promoting the growth of plants, which, in turn, produce trout food. Clear water also makes it easy for trout to see food and avoid predators, including fishermen.

A lack of adequate dissolved oxygen is rarely a problem in trout streams, unless the water is quite stagnant and high in organic pollutants. In most instances, oxygen is replenished through contact with the air.

In most streams the exact pH level is of little importance to fishermen. Trout, like most fish, can tolerate a wide range of pH levels, and can live in waters with a pH as low as 4.5 or as high as 9.5. But in streams near the low end of this pH spectrum, acidic water limits food production, limiting trout production.

Common Types of Trout Steams

Trout can be found in streams ranging in size from meadow brooks narrow enough to hop across, to major rivers large enough to carry oceangoing vessels. Following are descriptions of the most common types of trout streams, representing both the limestone and freestone categories.

SPRING CREEKS (left) arise from groundwater sources: They have slow to moderate current and very clear water. The stable water level allows development of lush weed growth, resulting in heavy insect populations. Some spring creeks produce tremendous numbers of crustaceans and surprisingly large trout. TAILWATER STREAMS (right) fed by cold water from the depths of a reservoir, often hold large trout populations, including many fish of trophy size. The best tailwater streams have stable flows, allowing development of rooted vegetation that holds many aquatic insects. Trout are not as numerous in tailwater streams where the water level fluctuates greatly as water is released to drive power generator turbines. These fluctuations limit insect populations and trout reproduction.

MEDIUM-GRADIENT FREESTONE STREAMS, are composed mostly of large gravel, rubble and boulders, and have some pocket water. These streams are fed mainly by surface runoff and meltwater. Because the water carries few nutrients, these streams are relatively unproductive. The best of these streams have many springs and clean, rocky bottoms that provide habitat for aquatic insects.

HIGH-GRADIENT FREESTONG STREAMS, fed mainly by snowmelt and surface runoff, are usually found in mountainous areas. The current is fast, with long stretches of pocket water but few pools. Because of the limited food supply, trout usually run small but are willing biters.

LOW-GRADIENT FREESTONE STREAMS wind through bogs, meadows or woodlands. They have sandy or silty bottoms, and undercut banks or deadfalls for cover. Some streams, fed by springs or meltwater, have clear water; others, fed by swamp drainage, have tea-colored water.

The Mechanics of Moving Water

Why does a trout lie upstream of a boulder when there is a noticeable eddy on the downstream side? Why does it choose a feeding lie on the bottom when most of its food is drifting on the surface? And why does a fly cast near the bank drift more slowly than the fly line in midstream?

Questions like these have a direct bearing on your ability to find and catch trout. Answering them correctly requires a basic understanding of stream hydraulics.

The trout holds on the upstream side of the boulder because an eddy forms upstream of an object as well as downstream. The trout chooses a feeding lie on the bottom because friction with bottom materials slows the current to as little as one-fourth the speed in the center of the stream (p. 86). Similarly, the fly next to the bank drifts more slowly than the fly line, because friction with the bank slows the current.

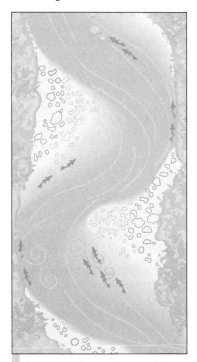

UNDERCUTS occur in meandering streams because current flowing to the outside of a bend becomes swifter, eroding the streambank. At the same time, current on the opposite side of the stream slackens, depositing sediment and forming a bar or point. In almost all cases, the outside bends and eddies below the bars and points hold the most trout.

CURRENT SPEED varies within the stream cross section. The light blue area (1) has slow current; the medium blue (2), moderate current; the dark blue (3), fast current. Water in the fast zone moves up to four times as fast as that in the slow zone. For purposes of illustration, the fast zone is depicted in the middle of the stream, but it could occur in any part of the stream's cross section, depending on the shape of the channel.

EDDIES form both upstream and downstream of a boulder. Many anglers do not realize that there is an eddy on the upstream side; they work only the downstream eddy, overlooking many trout. Eddies also form downstream of points, sharp bends, islands and obstacles such as bridge pilings.

PLUNGE POOLS form at the base of a falls as a result of the cascading water. Plunge-pool depth may exceed the distance from the crest of the falls to the water level. A dugout often forms at the base of the falls, creating one of the best trout feeding and resting lies in the stream, especially for large trout.

STREAM HABITAT TYPES

Understanding how moving water shapes the stream channel and learning to recognize the resulting habitat types improves your chances of finding trout. In most good trout streams, the current creates a riffle-run-pool sequence that repeats itself along the stream course. The sequence may be less noticeable in very large streams or streams with a very slow current, but the pattern is usually there.

Most trout streams also have other important kinds of water, such as flats, undercut banks and pocket water.

A deep, stagnant pool may hold several good-size brown trout, but rainbows and brook trout are more likely to be found in the faster water of a run.

THE RIFFLE-RUN-POOL SEQUENCE

RIFFLE – Shallow water; fast current; turbulent surface; gravel, rubble or boulder bottom. In big rivers, these areas are called rapids.

RUN – Deeper than a riffle, with moderate to fast current; surface not as turbulent; bottom materials range from small gravel to rubble.

POOL – Deep, slow-moving water with a flat surface; bottom of silt, sand or small gravel. Similar but shallower areas are called flats.

FAST WATER in a riffle excavates a deeper channel, or run, immediately downstream. As current digs the run deeper, the velocity slows, forming a pool. Because of the slower current, sediment is deposited at the pool's downstream end, raising the streambed and channeling the water into a smaller area. With the flow more constricted, the current speeds up, forming another riffle. The sequence then repeats.

Trout Lies

Trout take up positions, or lies, in moving water based on the way it meets a set of three basic needs. The first need is shelter from constant current. Trout cannot swim against a strong current all day any more than you can run uphill all day. Unless they rest behind objects that break the current, they would soon tire. But trout generally assume holding lies that are close enough to the current that they can dash out and intercept any food it delivers.

The second need is protection from predators. Trout prefer water that is rough enough or deep enough that predatory birds, such as kingfishers and ospreys, cannot see them on the bottom. They hold where some type of cover, such as a log, undercut bank or deep pool, lets them escape pursuit by other predators.

Small and even medium-size trout may risk predation by feeding in shallow water, far from any shelter. But you'll seldom find large trout feeding in the shallows, unless there is some cover that they can easily reach.

The third need is adequate food. This need often overrides the other two. Trout live by a simple formula: the food they eat must provide more energy than they expend getting it. Trout will fight a strong current if hatching, migrating or drifting insects suddenly offer enough food to justify the extra energy required. During a heavy hatch, trout may hold near the surface of a pool or flat and feed greedily, exposing themselves to overhead predation.

These three needs are what prompt trout to hold in certain water types, and avoid others. Whenever you look at a stretch of water and wonder where to start fishing, ask yourself, "Where does the water best meet one, two or even all three of the trout's basic needs?" That's where you'll find fish.

The photos on the following pages show you some examples of each of the basic types of trout lies.

HOLDING LIES

These are the most common kinds of lies. Trout find shelter from current and protection from predators in holding lies, but usually not enough food to sustain themselves. Holding lies can be found wherever the water is deeper than three to four feet and has some sort of obstruction to break the current. Find a spot like this and you'll nearly always find one or two trout in it. They'll be feeding opportunistically, taking whatever the current delivers to them. If you drift a submerged nymph or retrieve a wet fly or streamer past them, they'll most likely take it.

TYPES OF HOLDING LIES

DEEP HOLES appear as dark areas in the streambed. Trout move into holes to escape the current. The best holes have boulders or logs for cover.

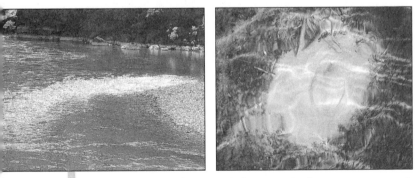

EDDIES (left) below points create slack-water pools where trout can escape the current. Some such eddies form reverse-current pools that hold many trout.

UPWELLING SPRINGS (right) appear as light spots of bubbling sand where the silt has been washed away. Because of their stable temperature, they draw trout in summer and winter.

FEEDING LIES

In these lies, trout find plenty of aquatic insects drifting along the bottom or swimming toward the surface for emergence, or they may find adult insects that fall into the water and drown. Some feeding lies provide a source of minnows, sculpins or crayfish. Because many feeding lies require fish to expend excess energy and expose themselves to predation, trout move onto a nearby feeding lie only when enough food becomes available to justify the switch. When the food disappears, they'll move back to the holding lie.

TYPES OF FEEDING LIES

POCKET WATER (left) is relatively shallow, with scattered boulders. It may appear too shallow, but the pockets and slots around the boulders often hold feeding trout.

CURRENT SEAMS (right) make good feeding lies; trout hold in the slower water at the edge of a seam and pick off drifting insects.

WEED PATCHES (left) hold trout because they harbor aquatic insects and crustaceans. The patches may be difficult to see, especially in low light. But the weeds usually slow the current enough to create slick spots on the surface.

OVERHANGING BRUSH (right) collects grasshoppers and other terrestrial insects, which fall into the water and become trout food. The brush also furnishes shade and overhead protection.

PRIME LIES

These are the best but least common lies – the areas where all three needs of trout are met in one place. Fish find shelter from the current, protection from predators and a constant supply of food. The largest trout in any stretch of stream will be found in its prime lies. Often a prime lie holds one big trout, which nestles into the most advantageous spot, and several smaller trout, which assume less desirable positions. Others include deep runs, plunge pools, brush piles, and root wads.

UNDERCUT BANKS can be found by watching the current. If it is angling toward a bank, rather than flowing parallel to it, the bank is undercut. Undercuts provide shade and overhead protection from predators and are magnets for baitfish.

BOULDERS provide shade and shelter from the current, yet trout can easily dart out to grab drifting insects and quickly return to cover. You can find boulders and other underwater obstructions by looking for the boil that forms just downstream as the current deflects upward. Remember that the boil forms downstream of the boulder, so you must cast upstream of the boil.

EMPTY WATER

The majority of the water in a typical trout stream has no productive trout lies. It simply fails to meet any of a trout's needs. It's important to recognize this empty water, so you won't waste time fishing it. Empty water may be just inches deep and very fast, with nothing to obstruct the current. Or, it might be slow and featureless, with a silty bottom that harbors no trout food and offers no cover.

SHALLOW RIFFLES, only a few inches deep, may draw trout at spawning time, but lack the depth to hold trout at other times.

FEATURELESS FLATS (left) have no boulders to create the pockets needed for trout cover. Trout would be easy prey for birds hunting in the smooth, shallow water.

STAGNANT POOLS (right) have no noticeable current and a very smooth, featureless, silty bottom. They often hold large numbers of roughfish, but very few trout.

Trout Foods

In the first few years of their life, trout feed heavily on immature forms of aquatic insects and, to a lesser extent, on adult insects, both aquatic and terrestrial. Other common foods include earthworms, leeches and small crustaceans, particularly scuds. But as trout grow larger, their food habits change. While they continue to consume all of these foods, bigger food items, such as small fish and crayfish, make up an increasing percentage of their diet.

Much has been written about the highly selective feeding habits of trout. But in reality, they feed nonselectively most of the time. Like most other predatory gamefish, trout are opportunists, taking whatever foods are available at the moment.

The tendency to feed nonselectively is greatest when trout are feeding beneath the surface. Then, they'll take most any invertebrate the current delivers. Ideally, it's best to match the size of your flies to the size of the naturals in the stream, but if you're not sure, use flies in sizes 14 or 16; these match up well with the majority of trout foods in most streams. Nearly all trout foods blend in with the bottom, so it pays to select flies in natural colors, such as green, tan or brown.

During a heavy insect hatch, however, trout may feed very selectively, ignoring everything but a certain insect form. When trout are feeding selectively, you don't have to match the hatch precisely, but you must imitate the size, shape and color of the natural more closely than you do when the fish are feeding nonselectively. For these occasions, it's helpful to have a basic understanding of common trout foods and their life cycles, as described on the following pages. Except for the larger stonefly species, which spend two years as nymphs before hatching, most aquatic insects hatch once each year. Variations in the weather and water levels can cause the exact hatch times to vary, but studying a river will generally tell you the right time to fish a particular fly. Take note of the calendar dates and time of day when you see insect hatches occurring, and file this information away for future reference. Fly shop owners and other fishermen often can be helpful, and river-specific guide books may contain information on typical hatch dates for insects.

The Stream Food Primer that follows shows the most common foods and a selection of flies that resemble them. Techniques for checking food availability in the waters you fish are shown on pages 108-109.

MAYFLY (*EPHEMEROPTERA*) LIFE CYCLE

Mayflies are the best known and most often imitated type of trout food among fishermen, and they've drawn the most intense attention of writers. The attention is well deserved, since mayflies are a very important food source for trout.

This insect order includes approximately five hundred species, which vary widely in size and color. Mayflies typically have a one-year life span, most of which is spent in the nymphal stage. When anglers speak of a mayfly hatch, they are referring to the emergence of the winged adult from the nymphal insect. Among aquatic insects, mayflies are the only species with a two-stage adult life phase. After developing functional wings, the adult insects molt their skins and transform from duns to spinners.

Blue-wing
Olive Nymph

SWIMMER NYMPHS are long and stream-lined, built for flitting through the water. They swim in short bursts and have two or three tails. These small nymphs prefer slow current and are most numerous in spring creeks, limestone streams and tailwaters. Use a size 14 to 18 fly.

Jacklin's March
Brown Nymph

CLINGER NYMPHS have flat bodies for hugging rocks in the fast current of freestone streams. The head is wider than the body; the legs, wide and flat. They have two or three tails. Although they usually live in violent riffles or pocket water, they migrate to quieter water to hatch. Use size 10 to 16 flies.

Hexagenia
Nymph

BURROWING NYMPHS have three tails, and may be more than 2 inches long. Some species have large gills that ripple in waves down their backs and give them an enticing action when they swim. Because they are burrowers, they live only in slower water where the bottom is composed of silt, mud, clay and, occasionally, gravel of pea size or smaller. Use size 4 to 10 flies.

CRAWLER NYMPHS are robust and blocky, with heavy legs and three tails. They crawl around on bottom rocks or in aquatic vegetation, but do not swim well. They adapt to a wide range of stream types, from rocky free-stone streams to weedy spring creeks. Use size 12 to 16 flies.

Dark Hendrickson Nymph

EMERGERS are similar to the nymphs in size, but appear to have a bubble in the middle of the back, which is created as internal gases build up to expand the wings. After the wings break free, the nymphal skin often remains attached as the adult struggles to emerge. Imitations should be approximately the same color and size as the naturals that the trout are feeding upon.

Goplin Emerger

DUNS have two or three tail filaments, depending on the species. In all species, the dun has two large upright wings, which are opaque. Some species have a set of smaller opaque wings. The body color and size can vary widely, depending on the species. Mayflies spend on the average of 24 hours in the dun stage before they molt again.

March Brown

SPINNERS, representing the final life stage of the mayfly, emerge when the duns split their skin. Similar in appearance to the dun, the spinner has two or three tail filaments and two large upright wings; some species also have a set of smaller wings. Unlike the dun, however, the spinner has transparent wings and its body is usually more brightly colored. After reproduction takes place, both sexes fall or land on the water – a moment known as spinner fall. Imitations should be the same approximate shape, size and color as the dun.

Red Quill Spinner

STONEFLY (*PLECOPTERA*) LIFE CYCLE

Stonefly species are present in trout streams throughout most of the country, and well-known stonefly hatches, such as the salmon fly hatch of the West, are responsible for peak trout and angler activity on many streams. Stoneflies require cold, clear, unpolluted waters, and because they cannot tolerate pollution or warm water, their presence can be used to judge the relative quality of a trout stream. Because most stonefly species crawl out of the water to emerge, the most important stage for anglers fishing the surface is the winged adult. Stoneflies offer substantial nutrition, and trout often throw caution to the winds when this meaty meal is available. The stonefly species have three life stages: the egg, the nymph and the adult. Most species have a life cycle of between two and four years; most of this time is spent in the nymphal stage.

ADULTS fly or crawl to a land area that offers them protective cover. Adult stoneflies have two tails, long antennae and four wings of equal length that lie flat over the body when at rest. Females deposit their eggs by landing on the surface of the water or flying just above it, at which time they are vulnerable to feeding trout. Adult stoneflies appear in one of the two positions on the water's surface. When the stonefly is at rest or dying, its wings are folded flat against the body. When it is laying eggs or is dislodged from streamside vegetation, its wings flutter. In adults, body colors may be tan, orange, yellow, olive, brown or black; distinguishing these colors is important to the angler choosing an imitation. Imitations range from size 2 to size 14.

Black Stimulator

STONEFLY NYMPHS hatch from eggs. The nymphal stage may last from two to four years, depending on species. They live in cold, clean, rocky, fast-moving streams throughout North America. The most important ones are 1/2 to 1 1/2 inches long, although salmonflies, found in the West, may be 2 inches in length. Stonefly nymphs have two pairs of wingpads, two antennae, two tail filaments and gills on the underside of the thorax. Most stonefly nymphs are black to chocolate brown, but some, called golden stoneflies, may be golden yellow with distinctive markings on the head and thorax. Use weighted nymphs in sizes 2 to 16.

Giant Black Stonefly Nymph

EMERGERS either crawl to the streambank or swim to the surface of the water, depending on the species. Most of the larger important species crawl onto rocks, trees or other objects near the edge of the stream to emerge. Swimming varieties emerge at the surface of the water, where trout may feed on them. When the nymphal skin splits and the adult emerges, leaving the skin, also called a shuck, behind, it pauses briefly to allow its wings and body to dry before seeking cover. Because emergence occurs on land for most species, this stage has limited importance to the fly fisherman.

CADDISFLY (*TRICHOPTERA*) LIFE CYCLE

Caddisflies are the most common aquatic insects in most trout streams and are more tolerant of pollution and warm water than other types of insects. Because caddis species are very widespread and can be found on just about any stream where trout are found, it's very important that anglers learn how to imitate them. Caddisflies go through a complete metamorphosis that includes four life stages: egg, larva, pupa and emergent adult. The complete life cycle averages slightly more than one year. The individual species vary greatly in appearance and habits, especially during the larval phase. Since the insect is the most vulnerable as an emerging pupa or egg-laying adult, these phases are especially important to trout and to fly fishermen.

CADDISFLY PUPAE are the intermediate stage between the larvae and the adult. They differ from the larvae in that their legs and wings are more developed. The pupae cut their way out of their larval cases and swim or float to the surface, aided by a gas that fills their outer skin. They hang in or just below the surface film until they emerge as adults. This usually occurs in riffles or runs. Trout feed more heavily on the pupae than the larvae because they're easier to find and capture. The pupae are usually cream, tan, brown, olive or orange, and there are two antennae swept back along the body. They are best imitated with flies in sizes 10 to 16.

Caddis
Pupa

CADDISFLY LARVAE hatch from eggs. Case-building larvae live in stick or stone cases, usually attached to the bottom of rocks. Free-living types, such as green rock worms, crawl though the spaces between stones in riffles, capturing and eating larvae of other insects. Some caddis larvae, called net spinners, weave "gill nets" that collect food particles from the current. Others, called tube makers, dig tunnels in the bottom. All of these larvae are wormlike, lacking wingpads and tails. Caddis are in the larval stage for about one year before entering the pupal stage. They vary in color from tan to bright green. Use flies in sizes 10 to 16.

Peeking Caddis

Peacock Larva

ADULT CADDISFLIES quickly emerge after the pupae rise to the surface of the water and split their skins. The mature insects quickly fly away, spending little time on the water, but will return several times to deposit eggs on the surface. Some species swim to the bottom of the stream to deposit eggs. Although they are very good fliers, adult caddisflies are vulnerable to surface-feeding trout. The adult's body is similar in color to the pupae. It has four wings that are swept back in a tent shape when at rest, and two long antennae at the front of the head. Imitations range from size 10 to size 18.

Tent-wing Caddis

MIDGE (*DIPTERA*) LIFE CYCLE

Midges include several thousand species of two-winged mosquitolike insects, including the tiniest of all aquatic insects. Midges are the most numerous and widespread insects in most trout waters, and are especially abundant in spring creeks, tailwaters, and slow-moving vegetated stretches of other streams. Like caddisflies, midges have four life cycle stages: egg, aquatic larva, pupa, then air-breathing adult. Trout feed on midges in both the larval and pupal stages, as well as on the adult insects. They may feed selectively on midges during a hatch and are more likely to take emerging pupae than adults on the surface. Depending on the species, the life cycle may be as short as a few weeks or as long as one year.

MIDGE LARVAE emerge from eggs. In some species, the larvae cling to vegetation or bottom debris, while in others the larvae are free-swimming. Midge larvae may have many different colors, but all are wormlike in appearance and are thinner than the larvae of caddisflies. You rarely need to use an exact imitation, because trout seldom feed selectively on them. Imitations generally range from size 14 to size 24.

Marabou Midge Larva

MIDGE PUPAE grow from the larval insects. Some species form cases during the pupal stage, while others actively move about in the water before maturing. The emerging pupae have noticeable bulges due to the developing wings and legs. Most species rise or swim to the surface to emerge, where they are suspended in or just below the surface film. Emergence into the adult form takes just a few seconds, but the emerging pupae are very vulnerable to trout at this time. Pupae imitations are usually some shade of black, tan, olive or brown and range from size 14 to size 24.

Brassie

ADULT MIDGES emerge and unfold their wings to dry while sitting on the surface of the water. They are most common in slower moving water. The adults have two wings, six legs and no tails. Coloration varies widely from species to species. Imitations for individual adults range from size 18 to size 26 for most species. Clusters may form when a group of adults are blown into clumps by the wind. When these clusters are available, trout are more likely to feed on them than on individual insects. Size 16 to size 22 flies are used for most midge cluster imitations.

Cream Midge

CRANEFLIES are one of the largest midge species. In adult form, the cranefly looks like a large mosquito as it skitters across the water to lay its eggs. Trout feed aggressively on the individual insects. Use imitations from sizes 12 to 16.

Brown Variant

OTHER COMMON TROUT FOODS

Many foods, in addition to aquatic insects, are present in the trout stream and utilized by trout. Terrestrials, or land-borne insects, minnows, crustaceans and other foods can make up an important portion of the trout's daily diet. The foods described in this section are some of the most common types utilized by trout in streams. Examples of flies used to imitate these foods are also shown, along with general information about the forage and the imitations.

ANTS are one of the most consistent terrestrial foods for trout – and ant imitations are one of the most productive fly patterns. Ants have three body segments, but imitations tied with either two or three segments are equally effective. Some imitations have wings and are designed to resemble winged ants. Imitations are available in black, cinnamon and varying shades of brown; and in sizes ranging from 12 to 22.

Foam Ant

GRASSHOPPERS will be eaten greedily by trout wherever they are available – most commonly, along grassy streambanks. Grasshopper colors include lime green, yellow, shades of tan and dark brown. Imitations may have wings, and legs that extend through the surface film in the same fashion as do naturals. Imitations typically range in size from 6 to 14.

Rubber Legs
Henry's Fork
Hopper

Black Beetle

BEETLES – both terrestrial and aquatic – are fed upon by trout. Most beetles are tan, yellowish, brown, olive or black. Most are quite small, but some, such as the June bug, provide a very big meal for trout. Beetle imitations generally range in size from 4 to 20.

CRICKETS are less plentiful than grasshoppers on most streams, but where available, trout eat them with equal abandon. Crickets have six legs; the two larger rear legs are used for jumping. Imitations are tied with black or brown materials to match the natural. Typical sizes range from 10 to 16.

Dave's Cricket

INCHWORMS are the larval stage of terrestrial insects, such as moths and butterflies. Inchworms feed on leaves, and are preyed upon by trout when they fall into the water. Inchworms range in color from bright green to shades of brown. Imitations are typically tied on hooks ranging from 10 to 14 in size.

Inchworm

JASSIDS, or leafhoppers, are powerful jumpers and are often blown into the water while leaping. Their bodies are elongated but still fairly wide. Although colors vary widely, they are usually imitated with a genuine or artificial jungle cock feather. Size and shape are much more important than color when selecting an imitation. Hook sizes ranging from 16 to 24 are typical.

Jassid

MICE and other small rodents provide one of the largest food sources regularly eaten by trout. Only the biggest trout will take these food items. Use mice patterns with wide-gap hooks in sizes ranging from 2 to 6. When tying your own pattern, use natural deer hair to create an authentic color.

Mouserat

105

SCUDS are crustaceans, more closely related to crayfish than to aquatic insects. But they share the slow-water habitat preferred by mayfly swimmer nymphs, and are often found around weeds. They are most abundant in spring creeks and tailwaters. They swim along lazily with brisk movements of their many swimmer legs and use their tails to dart backward. Most scuds are olive, gray, tan, pinkish or orangish, and can be imitated with size 12 and 18 nymphs.

Pink Scud

CRAYFISH are a favorite of large trout. Found in most types of trout water, they are most numerous on rubble or weedy bottoms with slow to moderate current. They have five sets of legs, with the first set being greatly enlarged to form claws, or pincers. Their strong, flexible tails propel them backward very rapidly. Crayfish vary widely in color, from dark brown to olive to reddish to bluish. Imitate them with size 4 to 8 flies.

Clouser's Crayfish

LEECHES have a slow, snake-like swimming motion that is irresistible to trout. When not feeding, leeches cling to rocks or sticks on the bottom or attach themselves to rooted vegetation in areas with slow current. Marabou patterns, such as Woolly Buggers in black, brown, gray or olive, make good leech imitations because the material has an undulating action in the water. Natural leeches vary from 1 to 4 inches long; imitations are usually tied for the middle of that range, on size 4 to 12 hooks.

Woolly Bugger

MINNOWS commonly eaten by trout include chubs, dace and shiners. Trout prefer minnows from 1 to 3 inches long, but big trout will eat much larger ones. Minnows live in all types of habitat, but most are found in fairly slow water in deep runs and pools. Bright-colored streamers in sizes 4 through 10 make the best minnow imitations and are usually fished in the same type of water. Around dusk and dawn, however, streamers work well for trout feeding in riffles or other shallow water.

Mickey Finn

Black-nosed Dace

Gray Ghost

Black Marabou Muddler

OTHER BAITFISH favored by trout include sculpins, darters and madtoms. These baitfish are usually found on clean, rocky bottoms, where they take cover around or beneath rocks. Dark- or natural-colored muddler- or matuka-type patterns in sizes 4 to 10 make good imitations; fish them across the tailout of a pool at dawn or dusk, and even at night.

Black Matuka

Olive Whit's Sculpin

Checking Food Availability

In order to select the best fly, you must know what insects the trout are eating. There is no need to identify the exact species of insect, but you must determine the size, shape and color. You could find out by checking the stomach contents of a trout, but that means you first have to catch one and, in checking, you will probably kill the fish. Following are some ways to determine food availability without checking stomachs.

TIPS FOR IDENTIFYING TROUT FOODS

CHECK (left) clumps of weeds for aquatic insect larvae and scuds.

PICK UP (right) rocks and check them for clinging insects, such as caddisfly larvae and stonefly nymphs.

EXAMINE streamside vegetation. Kick the grass and bushes that border the stream, and watch for any terrestrials or adult aquatic insects that may be present. This method may help you identify food sources that are not immediately obvious.

LOOK through binoculars to spot insects floating on the surface of the water. In many cases, you'll be able to identify insects at a substantial distance.

SEINE the surface by standing downstream from a spot where insects are floating, gathering them into the screen as they drift to your location.

SEINE for subsurface foods using a piece of screen or fine-mesh netting stretched between two sticks. Stand upstream of the seine and shuffle your feet to dislodge insects and other bottom organisms, which then drift into the net.

4

SUBSURFACE FLY-FISHING
TECHNIQUES

Approaching Trout

A successful presentation depends on your ability to plan and execute a careful approach, taking up a position where you can accurately cast a fly to a trout's feeding zone. In a good approach, an angler considers all the senses a trout uses to detect predators. Not only do trout have excellent vision and the advantage of the Snell circle (p. 67), but they can hear and feel your presence if the approach is sloppy. As a general rule, the shallower and clearer the waters, the more careful you must be when approaching. In choppy, murky waters, visibility is poor and trout are less likely to see you or your shadow.

If possible, take the time to plan your route while observing the stream from a high vantage point. Before you begin fishing, equip yourself with dull-colored clothes, vest and hat that match the general tone of the background. A khaki vest will look glaringly out of place if the river banks are covered with deep green vegetation. In very difficult trout streams, some anglers even wear camouflage gear. Also make sure your equipment is neutral in color and has no bright metallic surfaces that will reflect bright light onto the water.

As you begin your approach, adopt the attitude of stalking hunter in a prairie setting, moving very slowly and taking pains to stay out of sight of your quarry. Hide yourself behind rocks and streamside vegetation, and stay as low as possible. Use shadows to help hide your outline and prevent light from reflecting off your gear and into the water. Trout will be instantly spooked by any movement or suspicious shapes above the water's surface, because many predatory birds and other enemies approach from this direction.

STAY in shadows whenever possible. This way, trout are less likely to make out your form, and they won't catch a glint of sunlight off your rod or reel.

If circumstances allow, try to avoid wading into the water altogether, making your cast from the bank instead. If you do enter the water, lower yourself slowly, and wade in a slow, patient fashion to avoid grinding bottom stones together. Move very gradually to avoid creating wading waves – the small ripples that are pushed out in front of you as you walk through water.

The approach is one of the most important aspects of a proper presentation. If you can't get close to a trout without spooking it, your presentation will have failed before you even cast. It's also important to position yourself so you can land the fish if you do hook it.

AVOID making wading waves. They can put trout down in a hurry, especially in smooth or slow-moving water, or when you're wading downstream. In fast or choppy water, the waves are not as noticeable. If you wade upstream, the current prevents the waves from reaching the fish.

Fishing the Subsurface

It's easy to understand why subsurface techniques are so effective. Trout do the vast majority of their feeding beneath the surface, primarily on or near the bottom. They also do a fair amount of feeding in the mid-depths.

Trout nearly always hold along the bottom unless an abundance of some food form prompts them to feed higher in the water. Here's a simple rule: Always begin by fishing the bottom unless you see signs that they are holding and feeding at some other level.

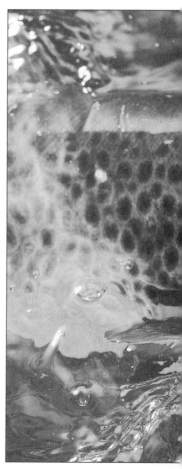

You may be able to spot trout on the bottom, especially if you wear polarized sunglasses. Look for anything out of the ordinary. Something that moves occasionally in opposition to the current, for instance, might be the finning tail of a big trout. A flash of white could be a trout's mouth opening to inhale drifting insects, or it might be a trout tipping its belly to the side as it takes naturals. A dark shape on a light bottom may be the shadow of a trout hanging invisibly a few inches above it.

Unless you can see them, it may be difficult to determine if trout are feeding in the mid-depths. But there are some good clues. Mayfly duns on the water, for instance, tell you that mayfly nymphs are emerging. If you see duns, but trout are not taking them, chances are they're taking the nymphs at mid-depth.

Trout sometimes feed in the mid-depths on caddisfly pupae swimming up from the bottom. The pupae are easier to catch than the winged adults, which fly away quickly once they reach the surface. When caddisflies are emerging, your clue is the splashy rises trout make as they chase pupae to the surface.

Most aquatic insects have drift cycles. At certain times, usually around dawn or dusk, great numbers of the nymphs or larvae let go of the bottom or weeds, allowing the current to carry them downstream. The sudden availability of food often prompts trout to feed heavily in the mid-depths.

On the following pages are the subsurface techniques most effective for fishing the wide variety of water types likely to hold trout.

Shot-and-Indicator Nymphing

This versatile method of presenting nymphs can be used in a wide variety of water types and forms the foundation of many of the subsurface fishing techniques that follow. Used primarily for covering the bottom when trout are scattered over wide areas, this technique can also be effective for targeting fish in specific lies.

The added weight ensures that your fly gets down to the bottom where the fish are most likely to be feeding, while the indicator, a piece of highly visible floating material attached to your leader, lets you monitor what your fly is doing.

The fly should drift naturally, with little drag, so it looks like a dislodged nymph drifting freely in the current. If you see drag on your indicator, chances are the nymph is not drifting freely. Depending on the current pattern between you and the indicator, you must throw upstream or downstream mends (pp. 62-63) to eliminate drag. To further ensure a drag-free drift, be sure there is some slack line between your rod tip and the indicator.

As the weight ticks along the gravel and stones on the bottom, the indicator may twitch slightly on the surface. Any sudden jerk or pause in the indicator, however, may signal that a trout has taken the fly. Learning to read the indicator is the key to becoming a better nymph fisherman. Once you become more proficient at detecting strikes, you may not need the indicator.

Ideal waters for shot-and-indicator nymphing are featureless runs from 2 to 4 feet deep with a moderate current. Here, trout may hold anywhere on the bottom and the angler must present a nymph systematically throughout the run. The technique is less suitable for slower water where the disturbance of the shot entering the water is more likely to spook wary fish. It is also less effective in heavy, fast water, where it may be difficult to get the fly to the bottom. There, the Brooks method (p. 145) would be a better choice.

EQUIPMENT FOR SHOT-AND-INDICATOR NYMPHING

The heavy shot and wind-resistant indicator make casting this rig more difficult than casting a simple leader-and-fly setup. The leader tends to hinge at the split shot and tangle easily, particularly when cast with a fast-action rod. A medium-action rod helps open your loops to prevent these tangles.

Use a long fly rod, 8½ to 9½ feet, for easier line mending. A weight-forward line is recommended for turning over the heavily weighted leader. It also helps load the rod more easily on the short casts typical of this nymphing method.

You'll need a leader that's long enough for attaching an indicator while still allowing the fly to get to the bottom. In typical shot-and-indicator water, an 8-foot leader is sufficient. For water deeper than 4 feet or in slightly faster current, choose a longer leader, up to 12 feet.

POSITION the indicator up the leader by a distance that is approximately twice the depth of the water in most situations. In slower current, place the indicator up the leader a distance only slightly more than the water depth; in faster current, about 3 times the water depth.

ATTACH the weight to the leader just above the tippet knot. Use only enough weight to get your fly to the bottom. For easier adjustments when using split shot, attach several small ones instead of one large one.

ADD an 8- to 10-inch tippet section. Anything longer allows the fly to drift out of the feeding zone at the bottom.

TYPES OF INDICATORS

INDICATORS include: (1) corkie, (2) synthetic yarn, (3) float putty and (4) twist-on.

FLIES FOR SHOT-AND-INDICATOR NYMPHING

POPULAR FLIES include: (1) Gold Ribbed Hare's Ear, (2) Muskrat, (3) Fox Squirrel and (4) Herl Nymph.

TYPES OF WEIGHTS

POPULAR WEIGHTS include: lead or lead-substitute split shot (left), twist-on lead strips (center) and moldable tungsten compound (right).

CASTING SHOT-AND-INDICATOR RIGS

Conventional fly casting calls for tight loops, false casting and high line speed for distance and pinpoint accuracy. But a shot-and-indicator rig requires a different casting style. Because of the added weight and indicator, the line is more difficult to control and tangles more easily. And if a split shot or weighted nymph strikes your graphite fly rod, it could easily shatter.

By using shorter casts, from 20 to 45 feet, and open-loop casting (right), you can keep the fly, weight and indicator separated to better control the weight and keep it from tangling. Keeping false casting to a minimum also reduces the problem. One way to eliminate false casting is to let the current load your rod at the end of a drift so you can make a lob cast (p. 120).

One of the difficulties many beginning anglers experience in trying to cast a shot-and-indicator rig is that the extra weight causes the line to hit the water when attempting to false cast. To prevent this problem, aim your cast higher than normal.

The two casting methods shown on these pages will make it easier to cast a shot-and-indicator rig.

HOW TO MAKE AN OPEN-LOOP CAST

STOP the rod crisply on the back-cast, then lower the rod tip slightly to open the loop and give the leader and shot plenty of room to pass the fly line. Allow the line to straighten completely before beginning the forward cast.

STOP the rod crisply on the forward cast, then lower the rod tip again to open the loop. If you hold your rod in the normal position at the end of the forward cast, the loop will be much tighter, increasing the chance of the line tangling or the weight striking the rod.

HOW TO MAKE A LOB CAST (WATER LOADING)

(1) LET the current take out line until all slack is removed and the current lifts the fly and shot to the surface. Pivot to face upstream. (2) MAKE a forward cast, lobbing the fly upstream. If you're having trouble lifting the heavy rig off the water, make a short tug on the line with your line hand as you make the cast.

HOW TO COVER WATER WITH A SHOT-AND-INDICATOR RIG

ESTABLISH a casting grid that suits the water you're fishing. In this situation, quarter your first cast upstream, to point 1, and allow the rig to drift straight downstream. Make additional casts and drifts at 2- to 5-foot intervals, to points 2, 3 and 4. Then, move upstream a few steps and repeat the procedure.

HOW TO FISH A SHOT-AND-INDICATOR RIG

QUARTER *your cast upstream of the water you want to fish. The shorter the cast, the more control you'll have over the drift of the fly. Your line should land on the water pointing straight toward the indicator.*

FOLLOW *the drift of the indicator with your rod tip. Mend the line as necessary to keep the indicator and fly drifting naturally. As the indicator drifts toward you, draw in slack with your line hand and raise your rod to lift line off the water (shown). This way, conflicting currents won't cause drag.*

PIVOT *downstream as the indicator passes your position. To prolong the drift, lower your rod (shown) and feed line through the guides. Wait a few seconds at the end of the drift to let the current pull the slack out of the line. Then, make an upstream lob cast, covering the water as shown on the opposite page.*

Hinged-Leader Nymphing

One of the toughest things in nymph fishing is knowing exactly where your fly is in relation to your indicator. Unseen currents can pull a nymph in many directions during a single drift, making strike detection difficult. Hinged-leader nymphing, an alternative to the standard shot-and-indicator method, helps overcome the problem.

The technique, best described by veteran fly-fishing guide John Judy, involves building a leader that forms a right angle and suspends the nymph directly below the strike indicator. This way, the fly and indicator drift in the same column of water, reducing the effect of conflicting currents, which, in turn, reduces drag. Because you need less weight than in standard shot-and-indicator nymphing, the fly has a more natural action. And with the fly directly below the indicator, rather than angling away from it, takes are much easier to detect.

Like shot-and-indicator nymphing, the hinged-leader technique is most effective for covering broad runs with even flow and a fairly uniform depth of 2 to 5 feet. It does not work as well in water of varying depths. When your line reaches a deep hole, the indicator keeps the nymph from reaching bottom. The technique is ideal when fish are feeding in the mid-depths, because the fly stays at a consistent depth.

Because of the long, right-angle tippet, this rig may be more difficult to cast than some other nymphing rigs. The techniques shown on pages 119-120 will solve most of your casting problems.

A HINGED LEADER keeps the fly drifting directly below the indicator, in the same current lane. With a standard shot-and-indicator rig (inset), the fly may drift in a different current lane.

HOW TO ATTACH TIPPET TO LEADER USING AN IMPROVED CLINCH KNOT

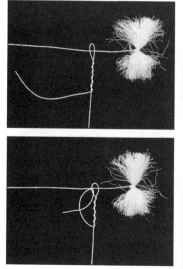

WRAP tippet (upper left) around leader, and wind tag end around standing end 5 times. PASS tag end through opening (above) closest to leader. BRING tag end back through loop (left). Then snug up knot by first moistening the wraps and then pulling on tag and standing ends. Trim tag.

EQUIPMENT FOR THE HINGED-LEADER TECHNIQUE

You can tailor a hinged leader to your fishing by adjusting the size of the indicator, weight of the fly and length of the tippet.

The indicator is made from a section of highly buoyant polypropylene yarn, such as Maxi-cord. High-vis colors, such as bright yellow or pink, are recommended. Carry a small pair of scissors to trim the indicator to the desired size, which depends on the weight of the fly and the turbulence of the water. Dress the indicator with floatant to keep it floating high.

Any type of nymph will work as long as it is weighted just enough to keep it drifting at a right angle to the indicator. A split shot is not normally used, but you can add one if necessary.

Use an 8$^{1/2}$- to 9$^{1/2}$-foot, 6- to 8-weight rod to cast the weighted fly and wind-resistant indicator and for easy line mending. A double-taper line helps you make the initial roll-cast mend, shown on pages 126-127.

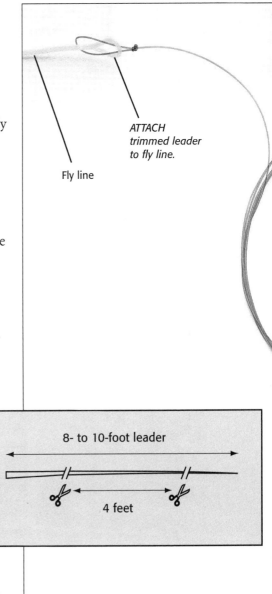

Fly line

ATTACH trimmed leader to fly line.

8- to 10-foot leader

4 feet

HOW TO MAKE A HINGED LEADER

CLIP both ends of a standard 8- to 10-foot knotless leader so it is about 4 or 5 feet long.

ATTACH a fan of yarn by wrapping the end of the leader around it and tying an improved clinch knot (p. 123). Dress the yarn with floatant.

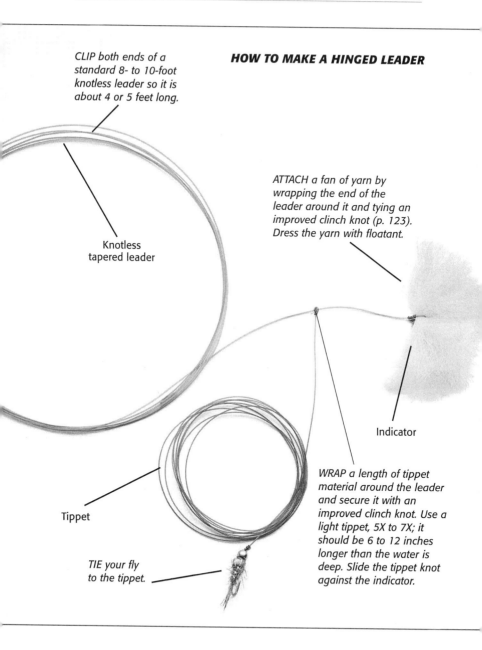

Knotless tapered leader

Indicator

Tippet

WRAP a length of tippet material around the leader and secure it with an improved clinch knot. Use a light tippet, 5X to 7X; it should be 6 to 12 inches longer than the water is deep. Slide the tippet knot against the indicator.

TIE your fly to the tippet.

125

HOW TO FISH A HINGED LEADER

QUARTER your cast upstream and across current. Keep your first cast short and gradually lengthen subsequent casts, as you would in the shot-and-indicator technique (p. 120).

MAKE a roll cast straight at the indicator. Called a roll-cast mend, this line-control method repositions the indicator upstream of the fly. This way, the indicator does not cause drag on the fly, allowing it to sink straight down and drift directly below the indicator. The mend should be just strong enough to lift the indicator off the water without lifting the nymph. The indicator will drift a little faster than the nymph; when it gets ahead far enough to cause drag, make another roll-cast mend.

LIFT the rod and strip in line as the indicator drifts toward you. This takes up slack between the rod tip and indicator. Maintain about the amount of slack shown; if you strip in line too fast and remove all the slack, the line will cause drag on the fly.

PAY OUT line to extend your drift as the indicator drifts past you. Set the hook at any hesitation or turn of the indicator. Make casts of increasing length until the section of water has been covered.

Weighted Nymph Technique

On slow spring creeks and smooth, clear runs of larger freestone streams, you'll often see trout holding and feeding on the bottom in water 2 to 3 feet deep. Drop a standard shot-and-indicator rig into the water, however, and you'll instantly spook the trout. A weighted nymph fished on a long leader is better suited for sight fishing trout on the bottom. The weighted nymph technique is not a good choice for fishing blind, because the extra-long leader makes it difficult to detect a take.

The long leader, 12 to 14 feet, keeps the fly line as far from the trout as possible, reducing the chances of alarming fish in the clear water. The tippet should be very light, 5X to 7X, for minimum visibility. On this rig, weighted nymphs in sizes 12 to 20 sink quickly and easily reach bottom with no added weight. To cast the long, light leader, use a 3- to 5-weight rod from 8 to 9 feet long.

When you see a trout feeding on the bottom, try to present the nymph within inches of its nose and watch for the white flash as its mouth opens to take the fly. If you're having trouble noticing takes, try attaching a small yarn strike indicator in a natural color. It will land softly, and the color won't attract the fish's attention.

HOW TO FISH A WEIGHTED NYMPH

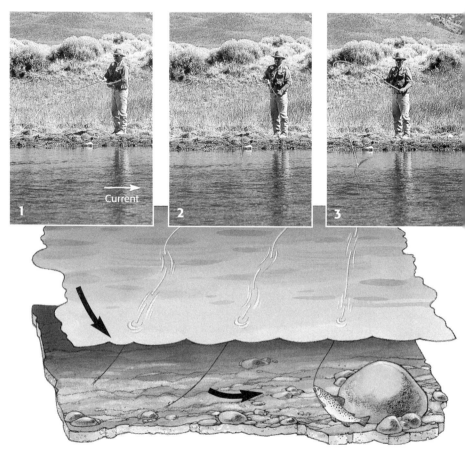

1. CAST from 5 to 15 feet upstream of a visible trout's lie, depending on water depth and current speed, to give the fly time to sink. False casts to measure distance should be performed sidearm, not directly over the trout.

2. FOLLOW the drift with your rod tip as the fly sinks to the bottom. Take up excess slack with your line hand, but don't draw the line so tight that it causes drag on the fly. Mend as little as possible; too much mending will spook the fish.

3. WATCH the trout closely. If you see a take, set the hook gently to prevent breaking the light leader and to avoid alarming the fish should you fail to hook it. If the fly is too far from the trout, complete the drift to avoid spooking it, then cast again. It may take several drifts before the fly arrives at the right depth at the right moment.

Upstream Dead Drift

A nymph or wet fly cast directly upstream and allowed to drift over a trout's lie can be very effective for imitating free-drifting food forms. The upstream dead drift also helps avoid the drag that results from casting across conflicting currents, because the fly line, leader and fly all drift in a straight line.

The technique is most effective in slow to moderate current from 1 to 3 feet deep. In most cases, you're casting to a visible trout or a probable lie, and this technique enables you to approach from directly downstream, so the fish won't see you. In narrow streams with heavily vegetated banks, this may be the only way of presenting a fly to the fish.

You can use the upstream dead drift to fish at most any level. To reach trout holding on the bottom, tie on a weighted nymph and cast well upstream of the lie so the fly has sufficient time to sink; add split shot if necessary. For trout in the mid-depths, use an unweighted nymph or wet fly, and don't cast upstream as far.

Casting upstream has its drawbacks, however. In clear, smooth water, the leader and line will fall directly over the trout, likely spooking it. To prevent this problem, use a reach cast (p. 132) to place the leader and line slightly off to one side. It also helps to use a long leader, 9 to 12 feet, with a 4X to 6X tippet. Even if the leader floats right over trout, they probably won't notice it.

Select a 4- to 6-weight rod from 7¹/₂ to 9 feet long. Rods at the shorter end of this range are best in narrow, brushy streams. Those at the longer end work better for making reach casts. Some anglers use a yarn indicator, which lands more gently than other types.

HOW TO USE THE UPSTREAM DEAD-DRIFT TECHNIQUE

STAND directly downstream from your target and cast upstream. When fishing smooth water, false cast off to one side and use a reach cast to keep the line from spooking the fish. If the surface of the water is broken, you can cast straight upstream without disturbing the trout. Cast far enough above the lie to allow the fly to sink to the fish's level.

TAKE up line as the fly drifts toward you to remove excess slack and allow you to set the hook quickly. Do not draw the line or leader tight, however, or the fly will not drift naturally. If you see the line twitch or feel a take, or if the fish suddenly moves toward the fly, gently set the hook.

LIFT your rod at the end of the drift so you can make a roll-cast pick-up (p. 134). This is the easiest way to pick up line when it is rapidly drifting toward you, and it minimizes disturbance on the water, so you won't spook the fish. When you have made several drifts in one location, move upstream or sideways to the next lie and repeat the presentation.

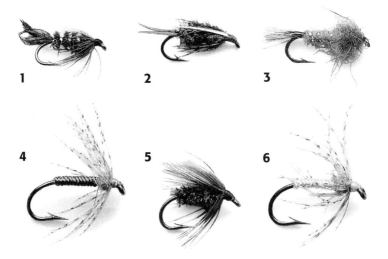

FLIES for upstream dead-drift technique include: nymphs, such as (1) Zug Bug, (2) Prince, (3) Red Squirrel; and wet flies, such as (4) Partridge and Green, (5) Alder, and (6) Partridge and Yellow.

HOW TO MAKE A ROLL-CAST PICKUP

RAISE your rod slowly as the fly passes the lie and while the line is still on the water in front of you. Stop the rod when it is slightly behind you (shown). Accelerate steadily, then make a short speed stroke.

STOP the rod quickly while the rod tip is moving in the direction you want the line to go. Let the fly line roll out in front of you; it should form an elliptical loop and straighten out above the water.

MAKE a normal backcast and then a normal forward cast or reach cast, and let the line, leader and fly settle to the water.

The Sawyer Method

Catching trout in the clear, slow water of a fertile spring creek can be a challenge to even the most experienced fly fisherman. Because they're so vulnerable to predators, trout are super-wary, and because food supplies are abundant, they rarely have to move very far for a meal. The late Frank Sawyer, riverkeeper on the Wiltshire Avon in England for over fifty years, pioneered the technique of sight fishing to trout in clear water with uniform currents. He discovered that by drifting a nymph directly to a visible fish feeding over a weedbed or otherwise holding in the mid-depths, he could induce a take.

The key to the Sawyer method is learning to read the speed of the current and knowing how quickly your nymph sinks. Then you'll know how far to cast upstream so the current will deliver your nymph precisely to the trout.

At first glance, this technique seems very simple, but it requires a great deal of practice to place the fly within inches of the trout, with no drag. The take may not be obvious; the fish just opens its mouth and sips in the fly, so you'll have to watch intently. Pay attention to the fish, but also watch the point where the leader enters the water. If the leader shows any unusual movement, gently set the hook.

This delicate method requires light equipment. Use a 7½- to 9-foot, 2- to 5-weight rod, a floating line and a 9- to 12-foot leader with a 5X to 7X tippet. You don't need a precise nymph imitation. A wide variety of impressionistic searching patterns, usually unweighted, can be used.

The Sawyer method is not a good choice in streams where the water is too turbulent to spot trout. Nor is it effective for visible trout on the bottom, because the fly will not sink deep enough.

FLIES for the Sawyer Method include: (1) Pheasant tail Nymph, developed by Sawyer to imitate a swimming nymph; (2) Quill Gordon Nymph; (3) Orange Scud and (4) Black Quill Nymph.

HOW TO USE THE SAWYER METHOD

POSITION yourself downstream and across current from a visible trout. Keep a low profile, using the streamside vegetation as camouflage. Cast far enough upstream of the fish so the nymph has time to sink to the fish's feeding level. Whenever possible, use a sidearm cast to keep your rod tip out of the trout's window of vision.

FOLLOW the drift of the fly with your rod tip. Watch the fish for any sign of a take, such as the white of its mouth or a sudden movement. You may have to drift the fly to the fish several times to entice a take. Set the hook gently so you don't snap the fine tippet.

The Leisenring Lift

Few nymphing techniques have proven as enduring as the Leisenring lift; and when done correctly, few are as deadly at taking trout. This method is equally effective fro sight fishing in slow, clear spring creeks and targeting obvious lies in freestone rivers with broad, even

STAND across current and slightly upstream of a visible trout or known lie. Cast far enough upstream to allow the nymph to sink to the fish's feeding level, 2 to 4 feet, before reaching the lie.

FOLLOW the drift of the fly with your rod, keeping the tip low. Mend the line as necessary to keep the fly drifting naturally (shown).

currents of moderate speed. The equipment and flies used for the Leisenring lift are very similar to those used for the Sawyer method. But because trout commonly feed on rising caddis pupae, caddis imitations are also effective.

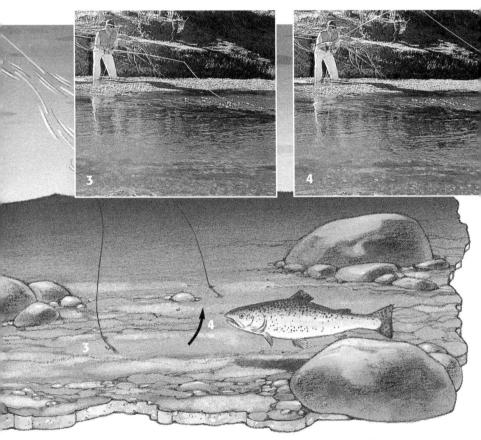

STOP the rod so the fly drifts to within about a foot of the trout or a known lie. The pressure of the current on the leader will begin to lift the fly.

LIFT the rod, if desired, to make the fly rise more quickly. When you detect a take, set the hook gently.

The Wet-Fly Swing

The wet-fly swing is one of the oldest techniques for presenting a subsurface fly to trout and is a longtime favorite among Atlantic salmon fishermen. Unlike other techniques, where drag is carefully avoided, the wet-fly swing actually employs drag to give the fly action and quickly cover the water. The force of the water on the line causes the fly to dart across the current, mimicking the action of a variety of food forms, including baitfish, immature aquatic insects and even terrestrials. With the fly passing crosswise in the current, the fish gets a good look at the side of the fly.

By controlling the amount of belly in the line, the fisherman can regulate the speed and angle of the fly as it swings across the current. The more belly, the faster the current will drag the fly. The pressure on the line also helps set the hook when a trout takes the fly.

The wet-fly swing works well in all types of water and current speeds, but is most effective at depths of 5 feet or less.

HOW TO USE THE WET-FLY SWING

(1) MAKE a short cast across the current to work lies that are out and downstream from you. The angle of your cast depends on the speed of the current. In swift water, cast slightly downstream to minimize the belly and keep the line from being pulled downstream too quickly. In slower current, cast slightly upstream so more belly will form, speeding up the fly.

(2)MEND your line to control the speed of your fly. If the fly swings too slowly, make a downstream mend (shown) to increase belly and accelerate the fly. If your fly is swinging too quickly, throw an upstream mend to reduce the belly and slow the fly. (3)LET the fly swing until it hangs in the current below you and begins to rise. You'll get a high percentage of your strikes at this point. (4)LENGTHEN each subsequent cast by 1 to 3 feet until you've thoroughly covered all the water you can reach from your position. Then, take a step or two downstream and repeat the process.

High-Sticking in Pocket Water

Among the most productive types of trout water are boulder-strewn, medium- to high-gradient streams with plenty of pocket water.

But pocket water can be very difficult to fish, explaining why it sees so little fishing pressure.

High-sticking can help you reach trout in pocket water. The technique involves making a series of controlled, short-line drifts, lifting your rod high above the water to take up slack as it forms. This keeps as much line as possible off the water so the current will not whisk the fly out of the pocket as soon as it lands. And with the current catching only the leader, rather than the whole line, the fly sinks more quickly.

In swift water, trout seldom move far to feed, so you must present the fly within inches of their lie. You may have to make as many as 10 drifts through a given pocket to cover it thoroughly. By taking up slack with the rod rather than your line hand, you maintain better contact with the fly throughout the drift, allowing easier strike detection and quicker hook sets.

Although you must get close to the fish with this technique, the turbulent water breaks up your silhouette. High-sticking will not work in slow, smooth water where the fish can easily see you approaching.

EQUIPMENT FOR HIGH-STICKING

An 8½- to 9½-foot rod is recommended for high-sticking. A long rod makes it easier to lift the line off the water to control slack. Since little casting is required, most any type of floating line will do. Use a leader from 7½ to 9 feet long so you can keep most or all of the fly line out of the water. The more turbulent the water, the heavier your leader can be. Use a 3X to 5X tippet in most situations.

A wide variety of subsurface flies, preferably searching patterns that represent a broad range of insect life, will work for this technique. Trout holding along the edge of fast current have little time to inspect your offering; they just dart into the current and grab it. In heavy water, choose a bead-head nymph or other weighted fly.

HOW TO COVER WATER WITH THE HIGH-STICKING METHOD

A strike indicator is seldom needed; because you are using such a short line, you are always in close contact with the fly, making it easy to detect a take. Most anglers just concentrate on the tip of their fly line. If you do use an indicator, however, it should be a high-visibility, high-floating type that shows up well in rough water. Attach it up your leader a distance approximately twice the water depth.

MAKE a series of casts to a boulder. Begin by working the side of the boulder nearest you, reaching out slightly farther on each subsequent drift, until you thoroughly cover the upstream and downstream pockets (white arrows). After working a boulder thoroughly, move upstream or out and work another boulder (black arrows).

HOW TO HIGH-STICK POCKET WATER

APPROACH the pocket from downstream and slightly off to the side, so the debris you kick up doesn't drift over the fish. Get as close as you can, preferably within 10 to 15 feet. Any farther and you'll have difficulty lifting enough line off the water. Make a short lob cast (shown), dropping the fly onto the water 2 to 5 feet upstream of the suspected lie.

RAISE your rod to take up slack as the fly drifts toward you. Lift as much line off the water as you can, but do not strip in line.

LOWER the rod as the fly passes your position to lengthen the drift. Let the current straighten your line at the end of the drift; then make another lob cast and repeat.

The Brooks Method

Originated by the late fly-fishing legend, Charles Brooks, this technique is ideal for delivering big, weighted nymphs to large trout in deep, swift water. Brooks, who lived just outside the town of West Yellowstone, Montana, developed his method on the famous rivers of that region. Brooks found that the largest trout hug the bottom

in deep, boulder-filled runs where the current speed approaches 8 mph. These big fish rarely move for a dry fly, and nymphs on light tackle do not get down deep enough to be effective.

The Brooks method is similar to high-sticking (p. 142) in its short-line approach and in the way line slack is controlled by raising the rod rather than retrieving it during the drift. But the differences are significant: short leaders, sometimes with added weight; sinking lines; and heavily weighted nymphs are needed in the faster, deeper water. Brooks even designed a number of fly patterns (p. 146) specifically tailored to heavy, turbulent currents.

An 8- to 9-foot rod, preferably an 8- or 9-weight, is recommended. Brooks used a 4- to 6-foot leader to keep the strong current from lifting the fly off the bottom, but you can go as short as 3 feet. A Duncan loop allows the fly to move freely on the stiff leader.

If you're after big trout in big water, the Brooks method is unsurpassed for getting your nymph to the bottom.

TIP FOR BROOKS-STYLE FISHING

CARRY a wading staff to help keep your balance in fast water with a bottom of slippery boulders. Wading boots with felt soles and metal studs (inset) give you maximum traction.

FLIES FOR THE BROOKS METHOD

POPULAR FLIES include: (1) Brooks Stone and (2) Skunk Hair Caddis, both designed by Charles Brooks. Other effective flies include: (3) Woolly Bugger and (4) Hellgrammite. The large flies, generally sizes 2 to 6, appeal to large trout, which usually ignore small food items because they're not worth the energy expended to get them. And large flies are easily seen in the turbulent water.

HOW TO RIG FOR THE BROOKS METHOD

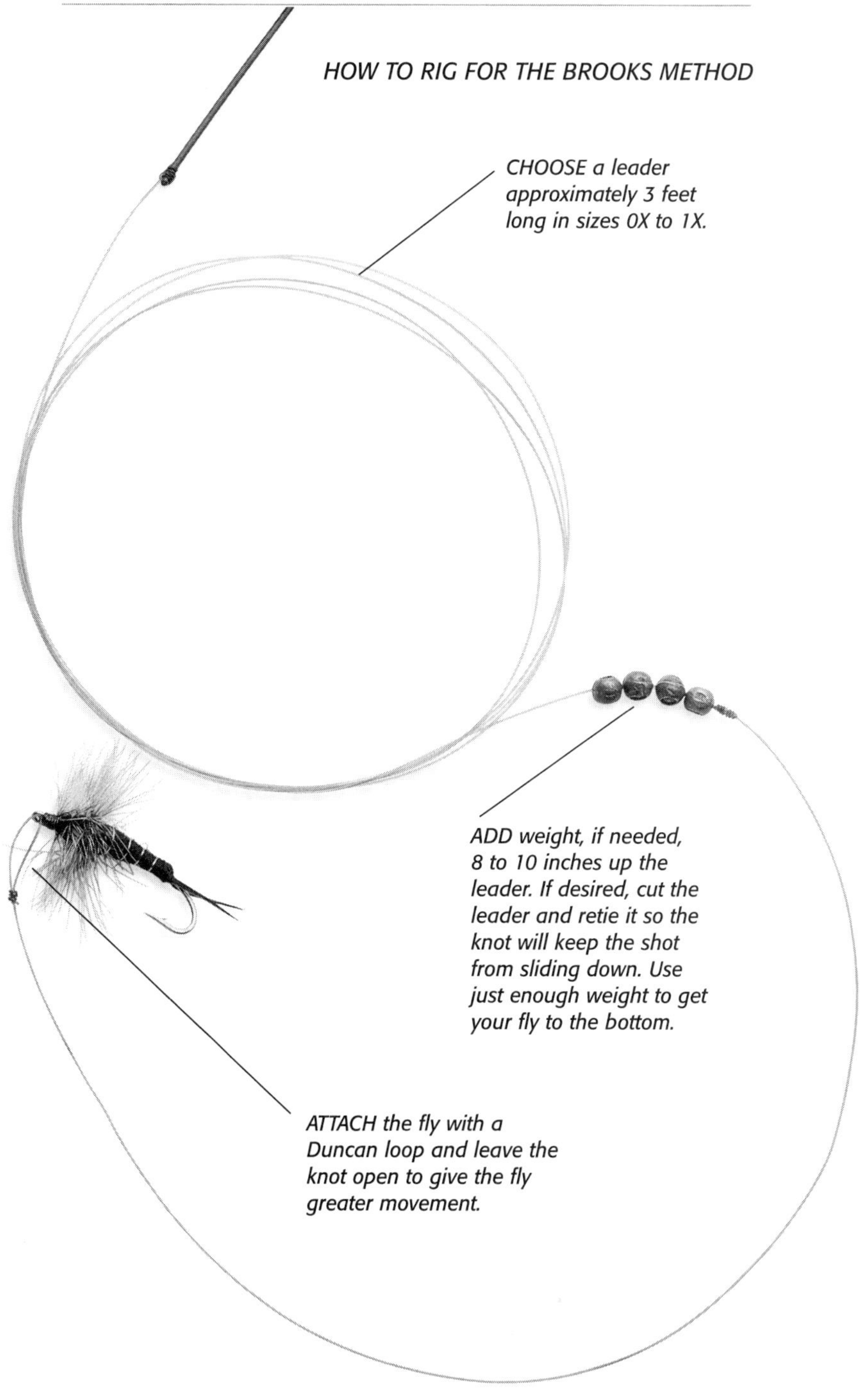

CHOOSE a leader
approximately 3 feet
long in sizes 0X to 1X.

ADD weight, if needed,
8 to 10 inches up the
leader. If desired, cut the
leader and retie it so the
knot will keep the shot
from sliding down. Use
just enough weight to get
your fly to the bottom.

ATTACH the fly with a
Duncan loop and leave the
knot open to give the fly
greater movement.

HOW TO USE THE BROOKS METHOD

LOOK for places where the fast water drops into deeper, boulder-filled channels. Stand 4 to 6 feet to the side and slightly upstream from the water you plan to fish. Cast upstream about 15 feet and about 6 feet out (shown).

AIM the rod tip above the point where the leader enters the water as the fly moves downstream. This allows the fly to sink; it should be on the bottom as it reaches a point 6 feet out from where you are standing.

LIFT the rod tip to take up and control any slack in the line, as you would when high-sticking (p. 142). The longer the cast, the higher you'll need to lift the rod. Do not strip in line with your line hand during the drift.

PIVOT slightly to follow your fly. As the line swings directly downstream from you, lower your rod tip to extend the drift. Wait several seconds after the line swings downstream. This eliminates all underwater slack, loads the rod and allows you to recast upstream, using a lob cast (p. 120).

The Deep Streamer Swing

When faced with a section of big, deep water, such as a wide pool or broad run, many anglers fail to cover every possible lie, bypassing numbers of trout. The deep streamer swing is the best method for sweeping a fly across the bottom of a broad reach of water to cover it thoroughly and work unseen lies. The technique is also valuable for fishing big, deep rivers, where you can wade safely only at the edges.

The deep streamer swing is similar to the wet-fly swing (p. 140) in that you're casting across-stream and letting the current swing the fly in concentric arcs through an area with many potential lies. The main differences are that you're fishing bigger water with heavier tackle and larger flies. And the flies are fished on the bottom, rather than in the mid-depths.

Large streamer patterns that imitate minnows, sculpins and leeches are commonly used, but the technique works equally well with big weighted nymphs, such as stonefly and hellgrammite imitations.

Most anglers use 7- to 9-weight sink-tip lines for handling the large flies and getting them to the bottom in the strong

current. Depending on the depth and current speed, use a slow to ultrafast sinking tip section from 5 to 24 feet long. In very swift water, you may need a full-sinking line; in a wide river, a shooting-head line. The leader should be short, from 3 to 6 feet, with a 0X to 3X tippet. A very long fly rod, 9 to 10 feet, is the best choice for making long casts with the heavy-sinking or shooting-head lines. This type of rod also makes line mending much easier.

HOW TO USE THE DEEP STREAMER SWING

Current

CAST perpendicular to the current and slightly upstream of the water you want to fish. How far upstream depends on water depth and current speed.

LET the current take the line downstream, following it with your rod tip. In slow current, you may have to make downstream mends to accelerate the fly; in fast water, upstream mends to slow it.

FLIES for the deep streamer swing include: (1) Woolly Bugger, (2) Spuddler, (3) Gray Ghost and (4) Hare Sculpin.

HOW TO COVER WATER WITH THE DEEP STREAMER SWING

MAKE a short cast from position 1 so the fly lands just upstream from the area you want to fish. Allow the fly to swing along arc A. Lengthen each subsequent cast by 1 to 3 feet, so the fly cover arcs B, C and D. When you've thoroughly covered the water from position 1, take a step or two downstream and repeat the process from position 2. Continue moving downstream until the entire area has been covered.

RAISE and lower the rod tip throughout the drift, if desired, to give the fly an erratic darting motion that will often trigger strikes.

153

The Countdown Method

First described by Ray Bergman in his classic book, *Trout* (Knopf, 1938), the countdown method is primarily a searching technique for helping you identify the level at which the fish are feeding. It is most effective in slow-moving pools, backwaters and large eddies, where trout may hold anywhere from the bottom to several feet above it. This water attracts schools of baitfish and, as a result, large trout.

As the name of the technique suggests, you simply cast out your fly, count while it sinks and then retrieve it slowly to keep it at the same level as long as possible. Use a hand-twist retrieve to mimic the action of a natural aquatic insect, or a slightly erratic strip retrieve to imitate baitfish or crayfish. If you feel a take, repeat the same count on the next cast. If you don't, keep adding a few seconds to the count until a fish hits. The countdown method is not well suited to fast water; here, your fly is quickly swept away, giving you much less depth control.

Bergman's original technique involved "blind striking," or setting the hook on a certain count, whether or not he actually felt a hit. Today, with more sensitive equipment, most anglers wait to feel a take before setting the hook.

Most any subsurface fly, including streamers, nymphs and wets, can be used with this technique. The type of line depends mainly on the water depth. In water no deeper than 5 feet, you can get by with a floating line. In deeper water, you'll need a sink-tip or full-sinking line, and possibly a weighted fly or a split shot, to stay down. With a floating line, use a 9- to 12-foot leader and a 3X to 5X tippet; with a sinking line, a 3- to 6-foot leader and a 0X to 3X tippet.

A 6- to 8-weight rod from 8½ to 10 feet long is the best choice for the countdown method, because it enables you to make long casts with a sinking line.

HOW TO COVER WATER WITH THE COUNTDOWN METHOD

POSITION yourself along the edge of a slow pool or eddy, and cast toward deep water. Count steadily as the fly sinks. When it reaches about 2 feet down, begin a slow retrieve. Be sure to work the shallower fish first; if you start deep, you may spook the fish that are holding shallower. Add several seconds to the count on subsequent casts, enough to sink the fly 1 to 2 feet deeper on each cast. Let's say you hook a fish there. You then fan-cast all the deep water you can reach from that position, repeating the same count. Keep increasing your count after thoroughly working that level. You may not find fish at some levels. But, as is often the case, more fish are found on the bottom. After working those fish, move to a different position around the hole perimeter, then repeat the same procedure.

5

SURFACE FLY-FISHING
TECHNIQUES

Getting Started

n many books on surface fly fishing, the term *presentation* is used to describe the various techniques used to cast dry flies accurately to trout in different fishing scenarios. But this limited definition ignores many important considerations that are just as crucial to successful surface fishing. Good casting techniques and line management are important aspects of presentation, but only in the hands of a competent angler who understands the entire process of presentation. In this section, the term presentation includes not only the cast and line handling, but all the preliminary steps leading up to the delivery of the pattern to the trout.

For our purposes, then, you could say that presentation really begins with developing an understanding of trout, their environment and their feeding habits – subjects that are covered in the third chapter of this book. Next, a good presentation requires that you know how to choose the right fly rod, fly line and leader. Another critical step in presentation is the approach – moving yourself into a position where you can make an accurate cast without spooking the trout (pp. 112-113). If you aren't able to get close enough, you have little chance of catching trout, no matter how perfect the rest of your presentation.

This section discusses some of the important preliminary steps in developing a successful presentation: the choice of equipment and general techniques. Then you'll learn the techniques for casting and managing line in a variety of fishing situations.

MUCH – perhaps too much – has been written about the importance of "matching the hatch": selecting fly patterns that precisely match the natural insects that trout are eating at any partic-ular moment. Identifying food sources and selecting imitations is a subject that can be as compli-cated as you want to make it – as any number of fly-fishing books have shown. But if you're more interested in catching fish than in identifying every species of insect in the stream, you'll be better off learning the more important aspects of presentation – approaching the fish, casting the pat-tern and managing the line. To be a top-notch trout fisherman, you don't have to memorize the Latin names of every bug.

Surface Fishing Equipment

The equipment required for fly fishing the surface is in many ways identical to that used for general fly fishing. When fishing the surface, however, it's crucial that you avoid drag on the line (p. 163), which can keep your presentation from looking natural to trout. For this reason, surface fishing with dry flies does require some special considerations.

LEADER

One item that is very important to the success of a surface fishing presentation is the leader. To ensure that your flies float without drag and look like natural food, it's crucial that the leader fall to the surface of the water with soft S-curves near the fly to provide slack. To do this, the leader must be constructed properly.

The function of the leader is to transfer energy from the fly line to the fly, causing the fly to carry past the rest of the leader before it drops to the water. The term "turn over" is used to describe this motion of the fly moving past the leader at the end of the cast. If a leader is too thick or stiff, it will transfer too much energy to the fly as it turns over. In this case, the leader will land in a straight line on the water, making a drag-free drift nearly impossible to achieve. On the other hand, if the leader is too thin or limp, it won't transfer enough energy, and the tippet will collapse on itself in a tangled heap without turning over at all. In addition, the overall length of the leader will affect how it turns over. All other variables being even, a short leader transfers more energy to the fly than a long leader.

Leaders can be built from many different materials, so it's wise to experiment with different brands and compositions. In general, the butt section and the adjoining midsection portion should be built with stiff materials, while the rest of the midsection and the tippet can be made of limper materials. In a typical leader, the butt section will comprise 35 to 45 percent of the overall leader length; the midsection, 40 to 55 percent; and the tippet, 10 to 25 percent.

Although there are many formulas for creating dry fly leaders, the basic leader that most fly fishermen use for surface fishing is based on the George Harvey formula. A leader built with this method will turn a fly over but still land on the water with slack in it. An example of a leader based on this formula is shown on page 162.

STIFF				SOFT		
			0X	2X	3X	4X
.017	.015	.013	.011	.009	.008	.007
10"	20"	20"	20"	12"	18"	22-28"

If you don't have the time or inclination to tie your own leaders, then you can, of course, buy them premanufactured. Modern manufactured tapered leaders, ranging from 7½ to 12½ feet in length, usually perform well with most surface flies. Since they have no knots, manufactured leaders won't pick up vegetation as do hand-built leaders. If you have trouble getting a manufactured leader to fall to the water properly, you may need to cut off the tippet section and adjust its length. Experiment with the length of the tippet to see how it influences the way the leader lands on the water.

In general, it's best to use a leader with the heaviest tippet appropriate for the conditions and fly you're fishing. A long tippet will allow you to deliver the fly a good distance from the point where the fly line hits the surface of the water, and will provide the adequate slack necessary for a drag-free drift. Long tippets are especially helpful on waters with tricky, conflicting currents. And a thick tippet, because it can withstand more pressure, will allow you to land your trout quickly – an important consideration if you plan to release the trout and want to make sure it's healthy.

Your choice of leader and tippet can be affected by the size and shape of your flies, on the stream and weather conditions, and on the behavior of the trout on a particular day. If you are fishing large, air-resistant flies, for example, you'll need a heavier leader and tippet to turn the fly over. Use the chart (opposite) as a guide for selecting a tippet size appropriate for the hook you're casting.

In general, light, thin leaders will be the best option in clean, smooth waters where trout have excellent visibility from under the surface. In other situations, however, you can get by with a short, thick leader. On days when the surface is broken by a stiff wind or dulled by thick cloud cover, you'll be able to fish a heavier leader. And if trout are feeding with indiscriminate abandon, a heavy leader is not likely to spook them.

UNDERSTANDING DRAG

Drag is the force placed on fly lines, leaders and flies when they are pulled across the surface of the water in a direction or speed that is not consistent with the flow of the stream. Typically, drag occurs when a floating fly line or leader has no slack to absorb current differences. When you cast across a stream to slower water near the edge, for example, the faster water in the center of the stream will quickly form a downstream bow in the fly line, causing the dry fly to be towed faster than the water surrounding it. Drag on the line causes an unnatural-looking wake to trail from your leader and fly, which will generally spook nearby trout.

Drag is most troublesome in areas of conflicting or variable current, and is one of the fly fisherman's most troublesome problems. The key to a successful presentation lies largely

TIPPET DIAMETER AND FLY SIZE

X-rating	Diameter	Breaking-strength Rating*	Fly Size Range
8X	.003"	1.0 - 1.8 lbs.	28 - 20
7X	.004"	1.1 - 2.5	26 - 18
6X	.005"	1.4 - 3.5	22 - 14
5X	.006"	2.4 - 4.8	18 - 10
4X	.007"	3.1 - 6.0	16 - 8
3X	.008"	3.8 - 8.5	14 - 6
2X	.009"	4.5 - 11.5	10 - 4

This chart is based on the actual breaking strengths of the materials used in popular tippet materials. Breaking strength on a given X-rating can vary greatly among manufacturers.

in your ability to eliminate drag on the dry fly and make it behave like a natural food item. Even though some live insects will skitter across the surface of the water, they rarely leave a visible wake. The wake left by a dragging dry fly, by comparison, is very obvious to trout, and such a presentation will rarely draw a strike.

Some dry-fly fishermen refer to a type of drag called micro-drag – minute movements of the fly imposed by the stream's current. These small movements are not easily seen by an angler, but they may be visible to the trout, especially in waters that are very clear and calm. In these conditions, your presentation must be even more precise.

Drag as a whole can be minimized with proper setup of the leader and by casting in a manner that provides adequate slack for the line and leader. It is virtually impossible to eliminate drag altogether, but it is possible to present the fly so it is drag-free for the short period that it drifts across the fish's feeding zone. If you master this ability, you'll catch your share of trout.

FLY ROD

Selecting a fly rod is mostly a matter of personal preference, so choose one that fits your casting style and feels comfortable to you. For general dry-fly fishing, a light 4- or 5-weight rod will handle most of your needs. Long rods are sometimes preferred for their line handling capabilities, such as mending, but a long rod isn't well suited for casting in a tight space, such as a small brushy stream. Because they give you more leverage, long rods do permit you to cast into the wind. For most anglers, an 8$^{1}/_2$-foot, 5-weight rod makes an excellent all-around dry-fly rod.

FLY LINE

Obviously, you'll be using floating fly lines for surface fly fishing. These lines have a coating that is impregnated with tiny air bubbles, making the line just buoyant enough to float in the surface film of the water. A buildup of dirt or oil on a floating line can affect the line's casting performance and may cause it to sink. For this reason, clean and treat your floating lines regularly with a quality line dressing.

An important consideration when choosing a fly line is the taper. For casting surface flies, you can use either a double-taper line, which has a long, centered belly and evenly tapered ends; or a weight-forward line, in which a short belly is positioned near the front of the line. Double-taper lines are the most popular because they cast well at short to medium distances and allow for a delicate presentation. Weight-forward lines work well for casting long distances, but because the weight is concentrated at the front, the line may create more of a surface disturbance as it falls onto the water. A weight-forward line is useful when fishing large, air-resistant flies, such as a big hopper imitation, because it helps turn the fly over as you cast.

The color of a fly line makes little difference in most fishing situations. However, some anglers find a brightly colored line easier to see when casting and managing the line, allowing for more accurate presentations.

REELS

Your choice of a reel for surface fly fishing is largely a matter of personal preference. You should, however, choose a reel that balances with the rod and line size you've chosen. You should also choose a reel with a drag and backing capacity that is appropriate to the size of fish you're likely to encounter. Larger fish call for a reel with better drag and more backing.

ACCESSORIES

Among the hundreds of fly fishing accessories available, some are essential, while many are gimmicks that appeal mostly to gadget fanatics who love to browse catalogs.

One essential accessory for surface fishing is a proper fly box. Choose a box that holds dry flies without crushing the hackles. A box with compartments is ideal, but over-loading it can tangle the flies and crush their hackles. And don't forget to pack fly floatant and desiccant powder. Floatants are available in paste, liquid or spray form (p. 32); when applied to a fly they help keep the hackles dry and ensure the fly will float longer. Desiccant powder is a drying agent that helps remove water from a "drowned" surface fly.

Seeing the Fly

When fishing the surface, it's very important that a trout angler be able to see the fly floating on the surface. First, seeing the fly allows you to detect drag and take steps to correct it. Second, it lets you achieve proper placement with your cast. When casting to rising fish, you must drift the dry fly right into the trout's strike zone; in some cases, missing by more than one or two inches will ruin your chances. Finally, seeing your fly allows you to witness the moment the trout strikes. The modern fly rod is made of very sensitive materials, well suited for alerting you to subsurface strikes, but since a surface presentation requires a substantial amount of slack in the fly line and leader, it's almost impossible to detect a strike by feel.

Wearing polarized sunglasses will immediately increase your ability to see your fly. Although most anglers wear sunglasses, believing they help see beneath the surface of the water,

polarized lenses also help with surface visibility. By reducing glare, polarized sunglasses make it much easier to pick up a dry fly moving through swirling current. Polarized sunglasses are available in many sizes and styles, including prescription lenses for eyeglass wearers. Side shields or wrap-around glasses keep light from reaching your eyes from the side and can also protect your eyes from errant casts and sharp hooks. Wearing a hat or cap can also reduce glare, provided the underside of the brim is a dark, light-absorbing color.

Fish as close as possible to your fly. Not only will the fly be easier to see, but you'll be able to present it more accurately. On the following page, you find additional tips to help increase your ability to see dry flies on the water.

ATTACH a very small strike indicator to the leader. Choose an indicator that is just large enough to see at your maximum cast distance, and attach it 2 to 3 feet up from the fly. After casting, watch the indicator instead of the fly, and use whatever casting or line-handling techniques are necessary to keep drag from pulling on the indicator. This method works well where the water has a broken surface, and in streams where fish are not easily spooked. In smooth water or around nervous trout, indicators probably won't be effective.

CHOOSE brightly colored fly lines. Bright colors will allow you to visually follow the line up to the point where it attaches to the leader. Though this doesn't necessarily let you pinpoint the location of the fly, it does help you estimate where the fly is located. Practice this technique at close distances to become familiar with the relationship between the fly and the line. When you see a rise in the general area where your fly should be, set the hook: in many instances, you'll be rewarded with a trout.

FOLLOW the leader with your eyes, from the fly line to the fly. Often, you'll be able to spot the fly by tracking visually along the leader. To improve visibility, you may want to grease the butt section of your leader so it floats better. If you still can't see the fly, watch the end of the leader; look for sudden downward or sideways motion, and set the hook at this moment. Occasionally, you may be fooled by drag, but often you'll hook a trout.

General Technique

O nce you understand the basics of presentation –
equipment, approach, seeing the fly – you're ready
to begin mastering the art of actually casting a dry
fly to a trout's feeding zone. Although there are a variety
of specialized techniques for casting dry flies in different
circumstances, some general methods apply no matter
which way the fly is drifted to the trout – upstream, across-
stream, or downstream. These general principles will be
discussed on these pages, while more specialized methods
are presented in following sections.

GET CLOSE. It's always best to approach as close as possible without spooking the trout. Control over your cast
and management of your line will be easier at close range.

Cast no farther than the distance at which you can accurately control your cast and effectively manage the line on the water. If you have the ability to accurately cast 50 feet and are able to achieve a drag-free drift, then approach to this distance. But if your practical limit is 30 feet, then don't try to make your presentation until you have approached to this distance.

ACCURACY is very important when fishing flies on the surface. Practice to improve both distance accuracy and right-left accuracy (p. 49). Pinpoint casting will keep your flies out of streamside vegetation and is crucial for those occasions when trout refuse to move more than a few inches out of their feeding lines.

PLAN YOUR CAST. Before casting to a rising trout, take the time to watch how the fish is rising. If the rises follow a rhythmic pattern, you'll want to time your cast so the fly drifts into the feeding zone at the moment the trout is due to rise for another morsel. When determining the moment to begin your cast, consider the time it will take the fly to drift to the feeding zone as well as the time it takes to execute the cast. When trout are feeding in this predictable fashion, they often are so focused on the food drifting their way that they won't even take the time to examine your fly before striking.

When using the basic overhead cast (p. 52) in most situations, your final forward cast should unroll above the water. The leader should straighten out roughly at eye level and fall gently to the surface. Lower the rod tip smoothly toward the surface as the line falls to the water.

In most presentations, the fly should land ahead of or up-current from the point of the rise. By placing the fly about two feet in front of the last rise, you can generally be assured that it will drift through the fish's strike zone. Remember that in smooth or slow water trout take their time studying food offerings before striking. For this reason, your fly will have to be cast farther ahead of the fish, and you'll need to manage your line to create a longer period of drag-free drift. But don't cast too far ahead of the rise, because this increases the chance that conflicting currents will create drag on your fly and ruin the presentation.

RIPPING line off the water will disturb the water and spook trout, especially in smooth, slow current.

KEEP FALSE CASTS TO A MINIMUM. False casts are usually a waste of time and energy. You can false cast in order to aim the fly line for the delivery or to dry a damp surface fly, but remember that the more false casts you make, the greater the chance for spooking the fish, especially if your casts go over the trout rather than to the side. In rough water, you can sometimes false cast without frightening fish, but in smooth water trout will frequently spot your fly line sailing overhead.

MAKE YOUR FIRST CAST COUNT. The first cast over a trout is the most important one. With each successive cast, you increase the chances of spooking the trout. When casting to a rising trout or to a lie, it's best to err on the short side with your first casts. If your cast is too short, you may be able to recast and and attempt a new drift; but if you cast too long, you may "line" the fish – spook the trout by dropping the fly directly over its head. If you make a poor cast, however, and the fish doesn't go down, go ahead and complete the drift-through using the proper technique for the situation, then cast again.

If multiple fish are rising, or if you see many possible target lies, always begin with the closest one to avoid spooking more distant fish.

COMPLETE THE DRIFT. Allow the line to drift well away from the fish – 5 or 6 feet below its lie – before you pick up the line and attempt a new cast. There's no way to accurately predict how trout will react to a blown presentation. Some fish will instantly swim away and won't be tempted by any continued efforts on your part. Other fish, however, will hold their positions, but will refuse to feed for a period of time. After resting, these fish often begin to feed again and may respond to a good presentation. If a fish doesn't change its lie after a poor presentation, chances are good you'll get another shot if you're patient.

After a misplaced drift, use care when picking up line off the water for the next backcast. Take every precaution to make your presentation behave the way a natural food item appears to a trout. Any unnatural action will alarm the fish and make it difficult or impossible to catch it.

Upstream Techniques

Approaching a trout from the downstream side and casting upstream is commonly considered the best all-round presentation method. Because a trout generally faces into the current while feeding, your approach and cast will take place in the trout's blind zone, where the fish is less likely to spot you. This is not a universal rule, however. A noisy approach or sloppy cast can very easily spook fish no matter where it comes from. And, if a trout is holding in a reverse-current pool, it may actually be facing you as you approach and cast.

RELEASE small amounts of additional line with each false cast, until you haul enough line out to place the fly a couple of feet above the rise. Keep false casts to a minimum and direct them away from the fish.

LOWER the rod tip to the point where the line first contacts the water, then begin stripping in line. This ensures that the tip of the rod won't tow the fly to one side or the other, creating drag. A high rod tip creates excess slack, making a hook set very difficult.

BEGIN stripping in line immediately after the fly hits the water. The goal is to strip fast enough to prevent excess line from gathering at the front of the line, but not so fast that you remove all slack and create drag on the fly.

GATHER the stripped-in line by coiling it in your line hand. Strip in line until the fly is well away from the fish or until the line is at a manageable length to begin the next cast.

An upstream presentation has several inherent problems. When casting straight upstream, for example, the leader inevitably will sail over the trout as you deliver the fly to a spot just upstream of the fish. If your distance judgment is less than perfect, the trout may spot the fly line. And even if your cast is perfect, the tippet will be positioned right in front of the trout's nose as it takes the fly. Many a trout has been lost because its nose bumps the tippet, pushing the fly away from the fish's mouth. These difficulties can be minimized if you direct your cast up-and-across. Wherever possible, try to avoid casting directly over a trout. If your upstream cast is directed slightly across the stream's current, the fly line and leader will be out of the feeding lane and will be less likely to frighten the fish.

In some cases, however, a straight upstream presentation is your only option. For example, if you're casting to a very narrow current seam with wildly varying currents on both sides, you have little choice but to cast directly upstream. An up-and-across presentation in this situation would almost certainly result in drag.

Another technique is the upstream reach cast (opposite page), which lets you present a fly to an upstream trout with little chance of "lining" the fish. The reach cast places the fly line and most of the leader to the side of fish – not directly overhead. The reach cast is one of the best all-around casts, used either alone or in conjunction with other upstream, cross-stream or downstream presentations. However, because the fly line may fall across areas with different current, it is more likely drag will occur on the fly.

In situations where many smaller conflicting currents are present within a drift, it is important that your presentation create slack through the entire line. In this way, the current can pull the line in different directions without transferring drag to the fly. One easy-to-master method for increasing the amount of slack in the line is the tug cast (p.177). Unlike other slack-line casts, such as the stop-and-drop (p. 181), the tug cast doesn't require that you dip the rod tip near the surface of the water – an action that can instantly cause drag if the current near the tip of the rod is faster than the water on which the rest of the fly line sits.

THE UPSTREAM REACH CAST

FALSE CAST to let out the proper amount of line. Make sure you have some slack left in your line hand. Stop the rod at a higher-than-normal angle, and point it to the right or left while the line is still in the air. Allow the slack to slip out through your line hand as the line settles to the water.

POINT the rod at the fly and begin to strip in line as you would with any upstream cast. Timing is crucial. Stripping in too fast puts drag on the fly, while stripping in too slowly allows extra slack to gather near the rod tip, making it difficult to maintain a direct connection when you set the hook.

THE STRIP STRIKE

HOLD the fly line under the index finger of your rod hand while managing the excess slack formed as the line drifts downstream toward you. This ensures that the line will be in the proper position for the strike. Strip in line (arrow) and lift the rod when the trout takes the fly. Hold the line under the index finger of your rod hand as you set the hook. This allows you to grip the line and prevent slack from forming after the hook set.

Casting with upstream techniques can also cause problems when you attempt to set the hook. Because the line will be drifting back toward you, following the stream's primary current direction, it is crucial that you manage the line to take up excess slack as it collects between you and the fly (p. 173). This will allow you to execute a good hook set. One method for setting the hook in this situation is called the strip strike (above). This technique removes a great deal of slack from the line as it forms, improving the likelihood that the hook will find its mark when you set it.

THE TUG CAST

THROW a slower than normal forward cast and aim it slightly higher than usual. Just as the line straightens out above the water, give the line a tug with your line hand – the amount and speed of the tug will dictate how much slack goes into the fly line.

ALLOW the slack along the entire fly line to settle to the water's surface, then begin to strip in the line, maintaining the proper amount of slack at the rod tip.

177

Cross-Stream Techniques

Fishing across a stream – at right angles to the predom inant current direction – is a challenge for any fly fisherman. In almost every case you'll be coping with currents that vary both in direction and speed. Good cross-stream techniques are especially crucial in a fast stream where fish are holding or rising in the very slow waters adjacent to the bank – a very common situation. In these circumstances, it's often impossible to find a downstream position where you can cast your entire leader and line into the slower current. The only way to achieve a drag-free drift when casting cross-stream is through proper line management.

The reach cast is one of the best methods for casting a fly across a stream, because it allows you to position the line either upstream or downstream of the fly, depending on the nature of the current. If you're casting across fast current to an area of slow water, reach toward the upstream direction to ensure that the drifting line doesn't overtake the dry fly too quickly. On the other hand, if you are casting the fly into faster current, you should reach toward the downstream direction so the fly doesn't overtake the line.

The water mend (p. 180), used in many presentation methods, is especially helpful when dealing with the varying currents in a cross-stream presentation. A water mend can be executed in either the upstream or downstream position, and it may be performed more than once in a single drift. In the upstream mend, used when the fly is drifting in an area of slower current, the line is lifted and tossed upstream of the leader and fly. This prevents the faster moving line from towing the fly and creating drag. In the downstream water mend, which is used when the fly is drifting faster than the line, the fly line is flipped to the downstream side to prevent it from slowing the fly and

causing drag. It's crucial that you perform the mend before drag begins; careful observation and timing are important.

An easy way to eliminate drag is to simply lift the fly line off the water when it is drifting over a defined current seam (p. 180). Since there is no direct contact with the water, the line can't pull on the fly. This technique works only if you can approach very close to the seam and can extend your arm and rod so the fly line doesn't lie across areas with different current speed.

When casting to rising fish in very fast water, the period of drag-free drift will be very short – unless you are able to create a lot of slack at the end of the fly line. The roll cast mend (p. 181) is one technique that places a great deal of slack at the end of the fly line, near the leader. The stop-and-drop cast (p. 181), sometimes called a puddle cast, is another way to create slack at the end of the line. With this technique, the slack occurs because the front end of the line collapses before it reaches the water. The stop-and-drop is one of the few slack-cast methods that allows you to be very accurate with the placement of your fly.

LIFTING LINE OVER A CURRENT SEAM

POSITION yourself as close as possible to the current seam. Place your cast above the rising fish or the suspected lie.

HOLD your fly rod out over the seam. This will prevent conflicting currents from pulling your line and creating drag on the fly. The line should come off the rod tip at a right angle to ensure that the weight of the line doesn't pull the fly.

THE WATER MEND

(1) CAST above the fish so the fly will drift into the trout's strike zone. Leave extra line between your line hand and the reel. Watch the line to determine whether it bows upstream or downstream. If it bows downstream, you will be mending in an upstream direction; if the line bows upstream, you'll be mending in a downstream direction. Make sure to begin your mend before the bow exerts drag on the fly. (2)FLIP the fly line off the water with the rod tip, using a quick, short semicircular motion. Allow the extra line between your rod hand and the reel to slip through your fingers.

THE STOP-AND-DROP CAST

BEGIN a forward cast, aiming higher than you would with a basic overhead cast.

DROP the rod tip to the surface just as the line begins to straighten out on the forward cast. This will create slack that will puddle at the front end of the line.

THE ROLL CAST MEND

CAST the fly across and upcurrent from the trout rise or suspected lie. Allow for a longer drift to ensure that you have the time needed to complete the roll cast. Then make a gentle roll cast that repositions the fly line without disturbing the leader or fly. Direct the roll cast into the water instead of completing the roll in the air, as you do with a standard roll cast. Repeat if more slack is needed for a longer drift.

Downstream Techniques

Though it's generally best to avoid casting downstream for trout, sometimes this will be the most effective or practical presentation. In some cases, for example, your only access to a stretch of trout-bearing water may be to approach from the upstream side and cast downstream. A downstream presentation can also make sense in situations where casting is difficult or impossible. For example, delivering a fly to a spot under a low, overhanging bush is virtually impossible unless you drift the fly from the upstream side. A downstream presentation can have other advantages, as well. After a downstream cast, the fly precedes the line during the drift, ensuring that the trout will see the fly before it spots your leader or line. And since the line drifts faster than the fly, drag problems are sometimes reduced – provided the current patterns are relatively simple.

You should recognize, however, that downstream presentations are usually rather difficult. Trout almost always face upcurrent, and to ensure that you remain well outside the trout's viewing window, downstream casts must be considerably longer than upstream casts. Managing the line can also be a frustrating experience, because your fly line will cross more current seams, making it difficult to achieve drag-free drift.

Setting the hook can also be more difficult with a downstream presentation. When a trout faces you, the motion used to set the hook tends to yank the fly away from the fish. For this reason, it's best to set the hook using a sweeping motion to the side, forcing the hook into the side of the fish's mouth. On longer lines, the tension exerted on the line from the water may also help pull the hook into the side of the fish's mouth.

One of the few times when a down-and-across presentation is preferred is while fishing from a drift boat. In fairly uniform currents, the boat tends to drift faster than the fly line and will slowly overtake the fly unless an oarsman works carefully to slow the boat. Quartering your casts downstream at an angle to the boat will provide a longer drift before drag sets in.

As with other techniques, a downstream cast must leave enough slack in the line to prevent drag on the fly. One cast that works well is the wiggle cast (p.184), also known as the S-cast or serpentine cast. The wiggle cast puts enough slack on the water to allow the fly to drift well past the rise before drag sets in.

A very basic method for presenting a fly downstream is the lift-and-lower technique (p. 185), which is especially useful in riffles and other rough waters. With the lift-and-lower, first make a forward cast upstream and past your target. Then, lift the rod tip toward you to pull the floating fly back in your direction. When the fly reaches a point just upcurrent from the fish or suspected rise, lower the tip of the rod to allow the fly to drift into the feeding zone. Though simple in principle, the lift-and-lower requires practice to master. The timing and speed of the back pull and dropping motion are critical in positioning the fly accurately.

THE WIGGLE CAST

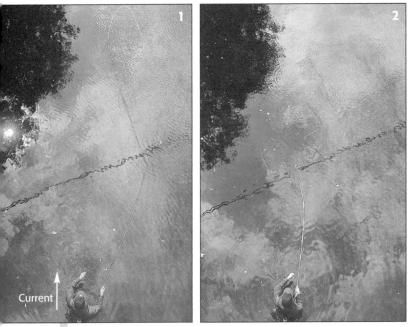

(1)MAKE a standard forward cast, but stop the rod at a point higher than usual, and immediately shake the tip of the rod back and forth. (2)CONTINUE to shake the rod back and forth as the line unrolls. The wider the arc made with the rod tip, the more slack you will get when the line settles to the water.

FEEDING LINE INTO A CAST

(1)CAST the fly above the fish, using a wiggle cast or another slack-producing cast. Lower the tip of the rod to a point just above the surface of the water, maintaining extra fly line in your line hand. If necessary, pull additional line from the reel before the cast. (2)WIGGLE the tip of the rod back and forth near the surface of the water after the line has settled on the surface, releasing the extra line in your hand. Surface tension will grip the extra line and form S-curves just past the end of the rod. Don't wiggle so hard that you create drag on the line already lying on the water.

An obvious way to add additional drift length to a downstream presentation is to feed line into the cast by peeling it off the reel and allowing the current to take it downstream. But make sure the current near the tip of the rod is pulling out the extra line; don't allow current to pull along the entire length of the line, because this creates drag on the fly.

Once the fly and two or three feet of leader has drifted past the fish, tip the rod to the side nearest you. The current will pull the fly, the remaining leader and the line to the side and away from the trout.

THE LIFT-AND-LOWER TECHNIQUE

(1) AIM your cast past the target spot and upstream from it. After the line is on the water, lift the tip of the rod straight back toward you, so the fly is pulled back in your direction. Don't lift too quickly, or the line will pull the fly under the water. Pull back until the fly is above the stretch of current where the trout is located, then allow it to settle on the water. (2) LOWER the rod tip smoothly as the fly drifts away from you and toward the rising trout. Lowering the rod too slowly will hold back the fly, creating drag; but lowering it too quickly will cause the line to pile up on the water – also creating drag. To drift a fly toward more distant targets, you can feed additional line into the drift.

Blind Fishing

Blind fishing is the practice of working a piece of water with a surface fly when you see no trout rising. Some fishermen enjoy the challenge of fishing in this fashion. Blind fishing may be very productive – provided the conditions are right and you know how to identify promising trout lies. Knowing how to read the water and understanding the trout's environment and behavior (pp. 64-93) will help you understand where to cast when fishing blind. Without this knowledge, you'll be wasting your time.

Blind fishing can be particularly successful and enjoyable when terrestrial insects are present, or in situations where fish are eager to eat any food source that presents itself. In general, waters that are rough and fast with limited visibility offer good opportunities for blind fishing, since trout in these conditions have limited time to inspect an item before striking. Though it's difficult to fish these waters without drag setting in, a lengthy drift is rarely necessary, since trout hit so aggressively.

Riffles and sections of pocket water are good places to blind cast surface flies. Because the flies drift past the trout very quickly, the fish may strike with little hesitation. Searching and attractor patterns, such as the Royal Wulff or Adams, are good patterns to use in these waters.

Since terrestrial foods present themselves randomly to trout, the fish are likely to take these insects whenever they become available. Even if you don't see trout actively rising to feed on terrestrials, the sudden appearance of a terrestrial insect – or a shrewdly chosen imitation – may create instant action. To improve your chances, cast to areas where trout might reasonably expect to see terrestrials in good numbers. Undercut banks with overhanging grass, for example, often harbor grasshoppers that fall into the water, so casting a hopper imitation into these waters makes good sense.

When selecting a fly for blind fishing, first consider the time of the year and the food sources available in your area. For example, a hopper pattern is not likely to work in a northern Rocky Mountain stream in March, but may work very well in August. When blind fishing, you should also choose patterns that can be easily seen, since this allows you to see if your casts have covered the lie. In general, large flies are easier to see, as are flies with light-colored wings, such as parachutes, wulffs and any flies with fluorescent wings.

Fishing at night, when you often cannot see your fly at all, represents the purest form of blind fishing. Occasionally you may be able to hear trout rising, but in most cases you'll need to cover the water in an organized fashion to ensure you're fishing over productive waters. Before going out at night, make a daylight scouting tour of the section of stream you'll be fishing. With this daytime image in mind, you'll find it easier to fish productively at night.

When fishing blind, approach the suspected lie with the same care you use when a rising trout is visible. Enter the stream at a spot where trout are unlikely to be holding, approach with stealth, and make your presentation as though casting to a rising fish. If you're fishing a terrestrial pattern, you may want to deliberately create drag to simulate the struggling of a grasshopper or ant. Cast to each spot two or three times, then move on to the next location. Without proof that a trout is present, don't waste your time by casting more than a few times to a single spot.

I N D E X

Creative Publishing international
is your Complete Source of How-to Information for the Outdoors

Available Outdoor Titles:

Hunting Books
- Advanced Turkey Hunting
- Advanced Whitetail Hunting
- Bowhunting Equipment & Skills
- The Complete Guide to Hunting
- Dog Training
- Elk Hunting
- How to Think Like a Survivor
- Hunting Record-Book Bucks
- Mule Deer Hunting
- Muzzleloading
- Outdoor Guide to Using Your GPS
- Pronghorn Hunting
- Whitetail Hunting
- Whitetail Techniques & Tactics
- Wild Turkey

Fishing Books
- Advanced Bass Fishing
- The Art of Freshwater Fishing
- The Complete Guide to Freshwater Fishing
- Fishing for Catfish
- Fishing Rivers & Streams
- Fishing Tips & Tricks
- Fishing with Artificial Lures
- Inshore Salt Water Fishing
- Kids Gone Fishin'
- Largemouth Bass
- Live Bait Fishing
- Modern Methods of Ice Fishing
- Northern Pike & Muskie
- Offshore Salt Water Fishing
- Panfish
- Salt Water Fishing Tactics

- Smallmouth Bass
- Striped Bass Fishing: Salt Water Strategies
- Successful Walleye Fishing
- Trout
- Ultralight Fishing

Fly Fishing Books
- The Art of Fly Tying
- The Art of Fly Tying – CD ROM
- Complete Photo Guide to Fly Fishing
- Complete Photo Guide to Fly Tying
- Fishing Dry Flies – Surface Presentations for Trout in Streams
- Fly-Fishing Equipment & Skills
- Fly Fishing for Beginners
- Fly Fishing for Trout in Streams
- Fly-Tying Techniques & Patterns

Cookbooks
- All-Time Favorite Game Bird Recipes
- America's Favorite Fish Recipes
- America's Favorite Wild Game Recipes
- Babe & Kris Winkelman's Great Fish & Game Recipes
- Backyard Grilling
- Cooking Wild in Kate's Camp
- Cooking Wild in Kate's Kitchen
- Dressing & Cooking Wild Game
- The New Cleaning & Cooking Fish
- Preparing Fish & Wild Game
- The Saltwater Cookbook
- Venison Cookery

To purchase these or other Creative Publishing international titles, contact your local bookseller, or visit our website at **www.creativepub.com**